OUR WOMEN IN UNIFORM

Editor - Muriel Stanley Venne
Lead Researcher/ Writer - P. Gayle McKenzie
Writer - Ginny Belcourt Todd

National Library of Canadian Cataloguing in Publication Data

Our Women in Uniform :

Honouring Aboriginal Women Veterans of Alberta / Aboriginal Veterans

Includes index.

ISBN 1-894255-28-3

1. Women Veterans - - Alberta 2. Aboriginal Veterans - - Alberta

3. Canada - - Armed Forces - - Aboriginal.

4. World War, 1939 – 1945 - - Veterans - - Alberta

I.Institute for the Advancement of Aboriginal Women.

E78.A34O87 2003 305.48'89707123 C2003-905309-1

Book Production & Distribution by:

Bunker To Bunker Publishing
4520 Crowchild Trail, S. W.
Calgary, Alberta, Canada, T2T 5J4

Printed in Canada

*Dedicated to all of the young
courageous Aboriginal women
who served during war and
peacekeeping times.*

PREFACE

The idea for this project began in Athabasca, just prior to Remembrance Day about six years ago. There displayed in the window of the Metis Local office was a beautiful photograph of Corporal Bertha Houle in her uniform, surrounded by red poppies and other memorabilia - her hat!

This was so captivating! Women like her were an exciting part of my own memories as a young girl. Mary and Verna Cardinal in their Army uniforms coming home to Whitford during their leave in the 1940's, I so admired them!

In 1998, when a young University Student Marilyn Adsit walked into our IAAW office the opportunity was offered her to record their stories and write the proposal to the Alberta Historical Resources Foundation. Marilyn was able to travel and interview the Aboriginal Women who served in the Forces. She recorded their stories, created a poster with their photographs and wrote an article that was published in the Aboriginal newspapers.

This sparked the desire of IAAW to find more Aboriginal Women who would tell us their stories and actually publish their stories in a book. This year, 2003 Gayle McKenzie enthusiastically accepted the offer of coordinating the second phase of "Our Women in Uniform" funded by the Museum Alberta Heritage Grants Program. Gayle travelled to the homes of the women to gather and write their stories. With the editing and writing of Ginny Belcourt Todd and the guidance of the Steering Committee their memories were recorded.

"Our Women In Uniform" reflects the dreams of these young women to defend their country. They give us a glimpse of their growing up, how things were during the war years, the courage it took to join up, the romance and toughness of it all. We are grateful to them for sharing an exciting part of the Aboriginal women's history of our province and our country.

Muriel Stanley Venne
President & Founder

ACKNOWLEDGEMENTS

Thanks to:

- Marilyn Adsit for writing the proposal, completing the first phase, interviewing the Aboriginal Women Veterans and writing the newspaper article.

- Alberta Historical Resources Foundation - funding First Phase.

- Museum Alberta Heritage Grants Program - funding Second Phase.

- P. Gayle McKenzie Co-ordinator for her enthusiasm and her excellent rapport with the Aboriginal Women she interviewed, her writing and rewriting.

- Ginny Belcourt Todd for writing the stories.

Members of the Steering Committee

- Victor Letendre President Aboriginal Veterans Society of Alberta - Edmonton, Alberta

- Donald Langford Aboriginal Vice-President Aboriginal Veterans Society of Alberta - Edmonton, Alberta

- Bertha Clark-Jones - IAAW Elder Veteran Air Force - Athabasca, Alberta

- Jan Roseneder- Military History Librarian Museum of Regiments - Calgary

- Ilona C. Cardinal for the cover of the book and formatting of the text.

INTRODUCTION

The Aboriginal women who made the decision to reveal their life stories for the sake of this book can only be described as brave and courageous, with an indelible pioneering spirit. Our research reveals that this book is unique in Canada; we could not find another book that was entirely dedicated to the Aboriginal women's experience as veterans, who served their country in war and peace keeping times. It was for this reason that the women, whose stories are told here, agreed to share some of the most intimate details of their lives with us. They all know how important it is to have a written record that shows that there were indeed Aboriginal women who enlisted for the main reason of helping to defend their homeland. They also know that theirs is a legacy that must be passed down so younger generations of Aboriginal woman have access to the finest of role models. It was indeed an honour and a pleasure to work with them.

The Aboriginal women's stories have been told in a way that reveals the loneliness, endurance, character, dedication, spirit, and sacrifices they experienced. They were unwelcome at first, in a world where men ruled supreme, but the times and situations of the day cried out for their support and they answered the call, willingly. They were in a way pioneers in a new world, who would by their work, their pursuit of excellence and an extraordinarily self-belief would forever change our society. The levels of self-achievement they attained were high in all aspects of their individual journeys. They not only survived, it can be said they flourished. They provided us with both a starting point and a benchmark

While each one of these women came from distinctive and unique back-grounds, with their own set of values and beliefs, they had one thing in common; they had very strong characters and a spirit that endured. They were all so young then, but they all had dreams of adventure, as they stood alone in times of civilian hostility. Being young and determined, they were not to be stopped from achieving their goals. They cultivated rich and lasting friendships with their comrades and went on together to develop a bond of sisterhood that they continue in their communities today.

No one can truly tell their whole life's story in great depth or completely describe all their feelings in a few short pages. However "*Our Women in Uniform*" has allowed them to share in their own words and is as complete as the women could tell of themselves. When the stories come together between the two covers, we the readers are given a unique view of a group of women who had faith in their country and in one another. They all stated they were proud to belong to the armed forces and to wear the uniform. There were all pleased to report that they suffered no discrimination from their comrades, most mentioned how the attitude of the public in general was very negative. In spite of it, or maybe because of it, they all learned how to interact with people and became great citizens and active in their communities.

P. Gayle McKenzie   Ginny Belcourt Todd

TABLE OF CONTENTS

ROYAL CANADIAN AIR FORCE
Women's Division

The Entry of Enlisted Women During the Second World War

Canada was at war

In keeping with the time honoured tradition; only men served in the occupation of keeping the home front free, so it was men and only men who were recruited for this duty. As men enlisted, were sent overseas and were wounded or killed, the Canadian military found this caused a new crisis to emerge. A labour shortage occurred in both the military and civilian job market.

Many women across Canada responded by swelling the number of volunteers who were already serving in that capacity. As men joined the armed services, women readied themselves to do "men's work" at home, some wanted to join the armed forces but government and public opinion would not condone the notion of a woman in the services, least of all a woman in uniform, submitting to the rigorous discipline of military life.

But the many women, who had resolved to join the ranks of men, in defending Canada, disregarded the notions held in all walks of Canadian life. They forged ahead by setting up volunteer organizations, which provoked some ridicule. They were not deterred; and created a way to offer training. It must be noted that they were fiercely patriotic and determined to serve their country. The final thrust to accept women into the Air Force came from the British Air Ministry when it requested permission to send their AirWomen to work on the British Commonwealth Air Training Stations in Canada.

Official Designation

By the middle of 1941 after much petitioning change was determined sparked by public demand and the necessity to free up men for services overseas. The need to train men as Commonwealth fliers continued to increase. Because air and ground crews were desperately needed, the Royal Canadian Air Force - Women's Division was given official designation on July 2, 1941. Within a matter of weeks, permission for the women's army followed, but women had to wait for another year before they could enlist with the navy.

At first, Canadian women joining the RCAF were actually enlisting in a separate entity-the Canadian Women's Auxiliary Air Force, modelled after the British Military's Women's Auxiliary Air Force. This was the first opportunity Aboriginal women encountered that would allow them to serve in the armed forces in any way. However, it only took a few months for authorities to decide that it would be more efficient to integrate the airwomen with the RCAF. As Aboriginal women writing this history we can well imagine how liberating it was for women to be given their chance to serve in a capacity that had been deemed by society, a privilege known only to men.

Requirements

After receiving basic training in Ontario, airwomen were posted to stations across Canada. Alberta was a popular place. Early recruits usually came with a trade: the minimum age requirement at first was 21 years old, with a year of post-secondary education. Later, when these age and educational standards lowered, trade school became a routine stop after basic training. Airwomen trained here and learned to be aircraft mechanics; cooks and physical education trainers, as telephone operators, stenographers, and drivers: they learned how to pack parachutes, took aerial and meteorological surveys; and performed aircraft maintenance. They learned communications, this included Morse code, radio transmissions and calculation of targets. Very few women were allowed to fly the aircraft. In all eleven trades were open to women. This number increased to sixty-five by the end of the war. Calgary and Fort McLeod, Alberta were two of the Canadian centres that offered wireless training. In spite of the training the women underwent to learn and master their chosen occupations they were only paid two-thirds, and later four-fifths, of the wages of a man doing the same job at that time Corporal Bertha Houle felt they were well paid, and was very proud to be able to send some of their wages to family back home.

Uniforms

The RCAF - WD had to design uniforms that looked feminine yet military, this was a problem through all of the services. The women were issued Air Force blue tunics, skirts, caps, greatcoats and raincoats, lighter blue shirts, black ties and shoes with grey stockings. Depending on the trade or rank they also wore the light blue smocks, overalls, dark blue cardigan sweaters, black gloves and overshoes. The summer uniform was a bit different. They were first issued blue cotton dresses, with nice gold buttons. Khaki coloured uniforms later replaced this dress. They were allowed an allowance of fifteen dollars to purchase their underwear. All of the women researched for this project declared they were proud to wear their uniforms. Most of the women had never worn such nice clothes and they didn't have to worry about what to wear. They were always dressed for the occasion. They became sisters in uniform. Their motto was " We serve that men may fly". More than one thousand women were in the RCAF - WD by the end of 1942.

The WD's in general were very active in sports, skiing, horseback and bicycle riding, forming basketball and baseball teams and travelling to compete with the other teams at different towns and barracks. They had to be physically fit to endure the drills and long marches; some marches were twenty-five miles.

Women in The Services

During the Second World War, between 1941 and 1946 approximately 35,000 Canadian women served in the armed forces, with over 17,000 serving in the Royal Canadian Air Force Women's Division. Some also made the ultimate sacrifice of their lives for their country. Thirty airwomen were killed while in active service. The division was disbanded and all women were discharged at the end of the war, but five years later, in 1951 The RCAF began recruiting again for the peacekeepers.

In 1968, the Minister of National Defense unified the Canadian Army the Royal Canadian Air Force and the Royal Canadian Navy. Men and women now served together in the new Canadian Forces. In 1971, the Minister confirmed that there be no limitation of the employment of women in the Canadian Forces. Women could now wholly serve their country in the military.

CANADIAN WOMEN'S ARMY CORPS.

Women in The Canadian Military

The Second World War was the first time that women truly became involved as participants in the history of the Canadian Military. This was important to women, as employment of female personnel would provide jobs that gave women a sense of purpose in a way that had never happened before. As one of the women interviewed said "joining up gave me the chance to do something else besides housework and get paid as well". Women had served in the military prior to the Second World War generally as nurses in arenas such as the Northwest Rebellion (1885), the South African War (1899-1902) and World War One (1914-1918). In 1938, when it became obvious that Canada would be at war in Europe, a woman's group was formed in Victoria, British Columbia and in Edmonton, the Alberta Women's Service Corp. to organize volunteers to train in auxiliary roles to aid men in the services. These young women, a dedicated group, underwent vigorous training to learn how to carry out many duties that included: first aid, military clerical duties and motor mechanics.

Their efforts were largely ignored until September 1939, when Canada actually went to war. It soon became apparent that the supply of male labour was diminishing as the Allied Forces experienced defeats. There were doubts held by both the Canadian government and the military, whether any woman could successfully engage in work that had long been exclusively done by men. Ottawa had to reconsider its decision to enlist women, because they were gravely concerned about the supply of man-power at a time when they needed to expand all the Canadian Forces. Ottawa decided that women could be used to replace men in non-combat duty. This would be the most realistic way to free men to serve overseas on the frontline. As a result of this decision, on August 13th 1941, the government gave permission for the formation of the Canadian Women's Army Corps (CWACs).

Thousands of Canadian women enlisted, all eager to serve their country. In the beginning it was made abundantly clear that they were being accepted only so the men would be free to do the more important jobs that involved active duty in hazardous conditions. Even though the majority of the women who joined the armed forces knew they would be performing duties well out of front line action, they enlisted for reasons such as: patriotism, new experiences, adventure and travel or simply because their friends or family members had already joined. The knowledge that they would be confined to the more mundane duties of military life did not deter them from enlisting as quickly as possible. They wanted to be involved.

When women first enlisted they were not taken as seriously as men. Societal notions regarding a "woman's place" reinforced the military and governments practices that war was a man's job. Women would be accepted on the premise that Canada was engaged in war, and that every Canadian should put forth every effort to help the men defend the homeland.

Women's entry into the military may have been taken lightly; but before their applications were accepted they had to meet the same physical requirements as the men; they had to be in excellent physical condition, at least five feet tall, and between 95 to 115 lbs. They were also required to have completed at least grade eight, be between the ages of eighteen and forty-five, and have no dependants.

Enlisted women found they were segregated by gender and were not accepted, or considered as a formal part of the army. They found their role was strictly supportive, therefore, were not subject to the same rules and regulations as were the men; they did not follow the same military discipline, rank designations, insignias, or general army practice. But it was a start. Women had made it in! It was one of the rare times, Aboriginal women who enlisted found they did not have to face or overcome racial discrimination; they were accepted as part of the military.

Women In Training

The enlisted women now had access to training that was not generally available to women, especially to young Aboriginal women. They were given training in supportive roles that included office work, drivers, messengers, cooks and quartermasters. At the same time, they were given an opportunity to acquire the skills, and knowledge that they would use as service women. They were indeed intelligent and able to carry out their duties efficiently and effectively. Through determination, and a strong work ethic their display of excellence slowly began to change attitudes long held by the military establishment that women could never be full military combantantss.

An indication that women were beginning to be taken seriously and looked at as a valued addition, was revealed when the army finally integrated the Canadian Women's Army Corps into the Canadian Army on March 13th, 1942. The change of mind was hastened by the fact that it made good sense for the military to integrate women, because running the woman's group of soldiers as a separate entity became an administrative nightmare. The integration gave the Woman's Corps new status and with it came army rank and insignia. The woman could now proudly wear their and display uniforms and display badges that indicated their rank and division.

Increased Self Esteem

Life in the army was an entirely new way of living. For the majority of women it was a lifestyle that was pleasant and at times quite exciting. All the women interviewed for "*Our Women in Uniform*" reported that they "worked hard, developed friendships and a comaradery that probably would not have occurred in any other setting". They had formed a sisterhood. Army life gave them the opportunity to serve their country, to travel, to meet people from all over the world, as well as other Canadian women. Many of them reported that being in the army made them proud. They were confident, healthy and in top physical condition. Their uniforms were great moral and self-esteem boosters as military personnel. The women developed a great sense of pride in both themselves and their country. The training they received would help achieve their employment and educational goals, once the war was over and they returned to civilian life.

Like the rest of the enlisted women, Aboriginal women suffered from unequal treatment that differed from that of the men. The women were aware that they played an important part in the war effort. They knew that if they were not there to fill in for the men, Canada would not have been able to send the vast majority of the men overseas. In spite of the crucial work that women delivered they were paid about two-thirds the pay for doing the same work that the men had done. One of the women interviewed said, "that's just the way it was back then, we had learned to accept it."

Treating women as less than equals when it came to wearing the uniform was not only a military notion, it was one that was generally held by Canadian society. The acceptance of women into the military was seen as a threat to the family unit and the break down of the home. It was difficult for women to be respected and treated as equals, when only "loose" women joined the forces, because all "decent" women with high moral standards knew their place was in the home.

Overseas and the Front Lines

Aboriginal women were given the same chance as all others to serve overseas. Most didn't, for personal and other reasons. In the summer of 1942 Britain requested that Canada send 350 CWAC's to their country.

The women who took overseas duty found that they were accepted by many of the Canadian soldiers. These soldiers lonesome for home, were pleased to be in the midst of Canadian women once again, while some of them saw the women as a threat. The threat came from the idea that the women would replace them in comparatively safe office jobs, while women would be put into dangerous war situations.

As 1943 ended, the women of at least three CWAC units found themselves in England. Once overseas, the women were given more responsibilities and duties because they had proven to be more than capable, and always executed their duties with deportment.

For more than a year, Canadian female soldiers remained doing clerical work in the England. Then in the spring of '45 the Canadian government made the decision that women could serve well behind the front lines of the war zone. The decision was made to send the women in, mainly because different headquarters were experiencing a shortage of clerical staff. For the first time women were placed in an area where they potentially could engage in war. For these first women who got to serve in the actual theatre of war, the time was short. Only a few months after their entry, on May 8th, 1945 Germany surrendered and in effect the war was over.

The Allied victory in Europe meant that the thousands of Canadian soldiers would be returning home. This would prove to be a complex administrative task that the CWAC could ably accomplish. Therefore, shortly after the war came to an end, hundreds more women were send to Europe to get the job done. Out of the nearly three thousand CWACs that eventually served overseas, none were killed and only four were wounded in Antwerp, Belgium. They had magnificently performed their duties. This Military experiment turned out to be a success. Many of the women wished to remain serving in peacetime, but it was not to be. The Canadian government disbanded the CWAC's on September 30th, 1946.

CORPORAL BERTHA HOULE
A Woman of Substance

Bertha Clark Jones received the Golden Jubilee Medal by the Governor General of Canada, commemorating the 50th anniversary of Queen Elizabeth II's reign, chosen by the Metis National Council September 27, 2002

Photo courtesy of Bertha Clark Jones (Houle)

Bertha Houle in full dress RCAF uniform, 1942. Top Left: RCAF insignia.

My Pioneering Family

I was born on November 6, 1922, the fifth child of fourteen. In my estimation my family embodied the courage, determination and pride that define the Métis Spirit. My father, Mr. Louis Houle, and my mother, Mrs. Emilie Houle, neé St. Arnault, raised their children well in spite of the many struggles they had to overcome. They were the same constant struggles that were simply a part of the pioneering way of life that faced most people of that time.

Magnificent Clear Hills Alberta

On October 13, 1914 my parents moved to Clear Hills, Alberta with their first-born child, only 13 days old. My sister made history by being the first baby to come to the area. They settled on their homestead in the new log home my father and his brother Albert had built for their small family. They were one of the first settlers to live in the district. Seven more children were born into our family during the time, every one birthed with only the assistance of mid wives, as there were no doctors located in the area. This was very common in those days.

Clear Hills was an isolated land of magnificent width, breadth and depth that challenged all who lived there. Our family found they had to surmount many obstacles that extended from harvesting the land to providing the basic needs for their growing children through the trying times of the great depression. They were barriers that could only be met by applying hard work and sheer determination. My parents did both so well and at the same time taught all their children the same values and work ethics. During these early years I learned many lessons from both my parents. They have, many times over, served me well throughout my life. By working hard and always going forward in spite of the difficulties we faced we were able to provide a good living for ourselves.

My Early Years

I loved the land of Clear Hills; it was created by splendid forests, lakes, rivers and streams for a variety of water fowl, moose, deer, beaver and many other fur bearing animals vital to the support of our family. Trapping and hunting were necessary because cash was hard to come by and there was nowhere to spend it, if we did happen to have money. This place is where I spent my childhood and early adolescence. I now know that my family and the land I grew up in helped to shape my character and, in turn, mapped out my destiny.

As a family member I had my share of household chores to do as well as a lot of hard outdoor work that involved caring for the garden, helping to keep the supply of wood and water going for the house, and roaming the land to hunt and gather food supplies. All the outside chores were left up to us older children to take care of as my father had to leave the homestead in the fall to go work on the trap line. He would not return until Christmas when he would sell his furs for the money that was needed to buy all the things in the Peace River stores that could not be made or grown at home.

A Special Christmas

Christmas was a special time of year for our family. The season was made all the more joyous because my father would be coming home after a long absence. He would bring all kinds of festive foods that included candies, nuts and armloads of gifts for everyone. I still clearly recall the excitement I always felt as the time of his arrival approached. One Christmas in particular my father appeared late in the evening. He told us that he had seen Santa Claus and his reindeer. I ran outside to carefully listen, and then actually heard Santa's voice calling out to the reindeer. I can still remember, as though it were a song in my heart, that call and the tinkling sounds of the sleigh bells ringing. It was a magical moment for me. I later found out it was my father's friend who was there to provide the voice and sound.

When father presented mother with a beautiful set of Blue Willow patterned dishes she too knew for sure that Santa was real. During the rest of the year I pretty much did what I was best at and what I preferred, "the outside work". I spent much of my time doing, as it was called then, "boys work". I loved this kind of work and the other activities that went along with it. My family and friends knew that I always did my work with a lot of high spirits. I also played the same way when I was either playing ball with my siblings and friends in summer or skating in the winter. My willingness to both work and play hard and enjoy every minute of it helped earn me the title of "tomboy".

The Handsome Uniforms

When I completed grade nine, at the age of 15, I went to work in the Manning Hospital and later on I went to live with my sister in Grande Prairie, Alberta. In 1939 I worked as a waitress in a restaurant, and also worked as a presser in a dry cleaning plant. It was not exciting work, but it was a paying job so I worked hard at it. We even did the laundry and dry cleaning of uniforms for the American soldiers who were stationed at Dawson Creek, B.C. They were building the Alaska Highway. I can still vividly remember watching the solders with gleeful exhilaration, their work looked so romantic and I was filled with a glorious enthusiasm and anticipation of what it would be like to be doing that work as a soldier.

Signing Up

In August 1939 we began to hear ominous rumblings about war in Europe. Although I was seventeen years old at the time, the spirit of the "Tom Boy" was still alive and well within me. I started to get the urge to go and do my part to help keep our country free. As a patriotic Canadian,

I wanted to be wherever I could be to help defend our country. Therefore, I decided I would like to join the Canadian Women's Army Corps (CWAC). I was thinking of joining up when it turned out to be a marvelous coincidence, there just happened to be a recruiting officer from the army coming to Grande Prairie looking for recruits. I went to sign up right away but I was told I was too young, a person had to be 18 before they would be recruited. I was bitterly disappointed, but not for long because only one year later, in November, when I had turned 18 years old, the Royal Canadian Air Force (RCAF) came to town to recruit. I once again applied to become a member and this time I was accepted. Soon after I joined with the RCAF, I received a letter from the army telling me that my application to them was accepted, but they were too late, I had already joined up with the RCAF. The year was 1940 when I signed on to the services and one year later my younger sister Christine Betsy Houle joined the RCAF as well.

My Stylish Wine Colored Hat

Soon after receiving my letter of acceptance to the RCAF I was ordered to go to Edmonton where I would have to undergo a physical and medical assessment. I did not waste any time getting ready to leave; I was more than ready to head out. So shortly after receiving my orders I found myself on a train heading for Edmonton. I remember being a little bit afraid because I had never been on a train before in my life and this was also my first long trip away from home. I was so fascinated that I forgot my fears as I watched the countryside fly by. It was great fun catching little glimpses into the lives of other people as we flew by them. The fact that the train was loaded with American soldiers made me a little more nervous than I might otherwise have been. I was not used to being around so many strange men and in such close quarters. The new outfit and the stylish wine coloured hat I had bought especially for the train trip gave me confidence. I knew I looked good from the many approving glances I got.

My New Uniform

As soon as I arrived in Edmonton, I was taken to the Air Force Base to undergo a physical and medical examination. If I had worried about the outcome of my assessment, I need not have been as I passed both examinations with flying colours. I knew I was in excellent physical condition because of my active lifestyle as a child and then again as a young woman.

Photos courtesy of Bertha Clark Jones Houle)
Top Left: Bertha saluting the memorial for WW I in Lethbridge.
Top Right: Bertha's jaunty little hat and new suit she wore to join the RCAF in Edmonton, 1942.

The next stop was the Clothing Depot, where I was issued my uniforms and they did the necessary alterations to fit me. The skirt lengths were very specific, as were the height of the heels of the beautiful leather oxfords that were a part of the uniform. We were issued two types of dress uniforms, one for summer and one for winter. All the airwomen wore the same uniform except for the officers of course; they had to wear the same colours, but made from a different material. When we were off duty and went into town we were required to wear our dress uniforms, fondly known as the "Air Force Blues". Various trades wore their official uniforms for work.

Basic Training

With my examinations complete and my new uniforms in tow I was sent to Ottawa the next day, for eight weeks of basic training. Again I traveled by train but this time it did not cause me any worry at all as I was a seasoned traveller now. It was the basic training I should have worried about. It was nothing more than I could handle but it sure turned out to be very rigorous with steady drills. They worked us without mercy for long hours and little sleep. Every muscle, even muscles I didn't know I had, ached like nothing I had ever known before. If I thought I was in good physical shape before I began my training, it was nothing compared to the new sleek and toned body I now possessed. I cannot say I was sorry when our training was complete, but I can say I felt like I could handle anything they threw at me now.

The Young Gunner

The first job I had in the air force was in the Airmen's Mess Hall as a cook's attendant, which lasted only a short while as I was soon promoted to the Sergeant's Mess Hall. I found that even working in a mess hall could be interesting and sometimes exciting. I had many new experiences there and most of them were a result of the person I was. One event occurred that I would never forget because having been raised in a large family I learned how to be a caring person who was always concerned for the people I lived or worked with. One day a young Scottish air gunner came in and wanted a vegetarian meal. The cook refused him, and told him he had to eat what he was served. This did not seem to be the right way to treat a person, so I tried to sneak food out to the young fella, but the cook caught me and threatened to charge me with insubordination. It was very windy the day this all took place and the plane the young gunner was on crashed. All were killed. I felt truly sad that this soldier's last meal was not the one he had requested. The memory of that day has stayed with me throughout these many years.

My Promotion

I enjoyed getting together to work and play with the many new friends I had made and to organize different sporting events such as playing ball games. My duties were varied and numerous but that did not stop me from putting everything I had into the work or play. I enjoyed most of it, especially the work in the sports department. My attitude was first-rate and must have made a good impression on my superiors because a sports officer noticed that both my friend Rose Makarenko and I were always vigorously involved in organizing sports events. As a result of his observations he recommended that we both take Physical Education Instructor's trades training. We did and after graduating from the course I became a Corporal. As a Physical Training Instructor I wore royal blue instructors slacks, white sweatshirt with RCAF insignia and white running

Top: Bertha's unit, 1943.
Below: Bertha's Physical Education Unit, where she was a Physical Training Instructor and played basketball regularly, 1943.

shoes. When we were playing basketball we wore the same uniform except for white shorts. Whenever I was not instructing, but still on duty, and left my area of work even to go for a meal on the base itself, I had to wear a royal blue tunic.

I remember how proud I felt on the day of my graduation when I overheard an officer remark that I had "excellent structure". As a Corporal, I was then put in charge of a whole squadron as their drill instructor. This position meant that I was to give instructional exercises to all personnel on the base.

Setting Eyes on Canada

When I joined up I had the idea that I would be able to see more of the world by going overseas, unfortunately this never happened for me at any time during my time in the service. When I look back I now realize that by staying in Canada I did get to see a lot of the country that I love. I was stationed at many different posts throughout this land such as Lethbridge, Alberta, Trenton, Ontario and Mossbank, Saskatchewan. I was also earning a salary. Wages were very low. Personnel in the armed services were paid only .65 cents per day. But out of this meager wage I am proud to say that I was able to send five dollars a month home to my parents who by this time lived on the métis settlement in Paddle Prairie, Alberta.

The Magic

Although there was a lot of hard work, there were also good times in the services. I often went to many of the social events that were provided for us such as dances, singsongs and sports. I made a lot of friends from all over the world. There was one young fellow in particular from the Royal Australian Air Force that I remember fondly. His nickname was Curly and I was very sweet on him. We had a lot of good times together until he was sent back to Australia after the war was over. Although I have thought of him time and again over the years, I didn't hear from him for fifty years, at which time our daughter arranged for Curly and I to meet again in San Diego, USA. As I watched him cross the airport floor I was amazed to realize by the pounding in my heart and the weakness in my knees that even after fifty years the magic was still there! I am so sorry to say that I found out at the time of our meeting Curly had cancer and passed away soon after our meeting.

Working Together

One of the best things about being a part of the services is that I never once felt any sort discrimination in the air force, it did not seem to matter that I was young, Aboriginal or a woman. I believe all enlisted personnel were treated as equals by everyone involved. This was the way it was because we had formed a bond that came about from working closely together as a team and sharing the same beliefs and values about what we were fighting for. Aside from that everyone was too busy and as every extra hand was needed there was no time or place for discriminatory practices. However, I did notice that the First Nations Peoples lost their Status when they left the reserves to join up, and this in turn, meant they did not have any land or houses when they returned. I was one of the lucky ones because I had a good counsellor when I was eventually discharged from the RCAF. I was offered a chance to go to university to complete a Physical Education Teaching degree, but I chose to go into Hairdressing, and the services paid for it. Today I can look back fondly to the years I spent in the service; it was memorable and an incredibly positive experience for me. When I left I took with me a higher degree of education and many practical skills, knowledge and abilities to forge a great life for myself as a private citizen.

Honourable Discharge

The Veteran's Land Act entitled me to receive ½ section of land because I had received a honourable discharge. I could choose any unoccupied Crown land to locate my ½ section on. I wanted to live in the Paddle Prairie Settlement, but was refused because women couldn't own land on the settlement in those days. This was an incredible disappointment to me for two reasons, first I was suddenly faced with discrimination from my own people because I was a woman and secondly because I could not locate near my father to help him farm and use my gratuities from the air force to help him. My parents were poor; I wished I could have helped them more. Instead I chose land that was located in the Peace Country at Hawk Hills north of Manning, Alberta.

Still Serving My Country

Today, more than 50 years have passed since the glorious days of serving my country; it is so hard to believe because the memories are still so vivid. I am an active community member now in Athabasca, Alberta. This is where I like to devote my time serving my country in other ways as a very active volunteer. It is an honour to be recognized as an Elder in the Metis community, and I am especially interested in working for all children so they may have a better future. I am a board member of the Child and Family Services Authority for the Province of Alberta. I do this because as a veteran I know our children are the future of our country and by working with and for them, the result will be a better world. In this way may we never experience war again.

LEADING AIR CRAFT WOMAN
BETSY HOULE

The Adventuress

RCAF insignia

Photo courtesy Bertha Houle (Clark Jones)
Betsy Houle, Grande Prairie 1944.

Growing up in Northern Alberta

October 17th, 1924 was the day of my birth. I was born in a time when
Metis people had large families in Canada (we had fourteen children in
ours). My parents Louis and Emily Houle, nee St. Arnault, reared us all
in a really big, house on our farm in Clear Hills, Alberta. Life was good
back then as we all enjoyed and endured the everlasting ups and downs
that seemed to occur when large numbers of people share their lives so
closely. My parents were pioneers who were not afraid of hard work and
knew how to take advantage of whatever leisure time we had earned to
provide us with the best homemade fun and entertainment. Father was a
great violin player and proved it at the end of the workday when he would
bring out his fiddle to play countless old Metis fiddle tunes. I believe he
knew them all, and he would play them for us children to dance to. In
this way we all learned how to dance as we learned to walk. Our house
was very large so my parents' hosted community dances there quite often.
There were few dance halls in remote farming areas and the mode of

Photo courtesy Bertha Houle (Clark Jones)

Back row: CPL. Bertha Houle, Brother Max Flavian Houle, LAW Betsy Houle. Seated: Sisters Stella Houle and Agnes HOule, Grande Prairie 1944.

transportation was a lot slower at that time. Our house was closer so as a result everyone would come to our house to celebrate special days with dancing and visiting.

Farm Life

Our farm was located in an area that was so beautiful it was like living in a park that offered a lot of recreational activities for children. We all had a lot of work to do both inside and outside the house, rearing a large family by farming is a demanding business, there was never a shortage of work every day. I especially enjoyed doing the outdoor chores with my sister Bertha. I guess we were both tomboys, but Bertha was the daredevil. I remember one time, we pretended to have a rodeo along with the neighbour's kids. It was on a Sunday and our parents weren't home. One of the older brothers lassoed a calf, and someone dared Bertha to ride the calf; never one to pass up a dare she jumped up on it's back. She did not have time to properly seat herself when the rope slipped and she ended up under the calf's belly. Even so she still wouldn't let go. The calf raced around the barnyard with Bertha under it's belly and all of us kids were yelling at her to let go. She finally did; fortunately she didn't get hurt.

School Life

Like the rest of the children I went to the Beaton Creek School in Clearhills for three or four years, until the time my parents moved the family onto a new homestead north of Clearhills, Alberta. After the move we attended a school called Golden Ridge where I remained until I completed grade eight. We then moved to Notikewin, in the Manning area; a good move for my parents in terms of business, but not so good for the children who wanted to attend high school as there wasn't one located in the nearby area. So my dad rented a farm miles away from the new one just so my brothers, my sisters and I could attain a higher-grade level. He did this because education was very important to him, as he never had the opportunity to go to school in his lifetime. In my mid-teens I moved to Grande Prairie, Alberta to attend school and live with my sister Agnes and her husband Phil Lessoway. I was taking grade eleven by correspondence at the same time that I was a college student taking bookkeeping, typing and shorthand. I applied myself to my studies diligently because I wanted to work in an office. However, I readily dropped it all when I got the opportunity to join the Armed Forces.

Young People Joining Up

Many of the young people were leaving Grande Prairie; I sure didn't want to be the only one left behind. I was eighteen years old and knew for sure this would be the adventure I had only dreamed of. I had also dreamed of travelling to distant places and I knew I would be able to continue with my education once I was in the service of my country. So a few of my friends and I went by train to Calgary where we enlisted. I was so happy because it was the most exciting thing I had ever done and at the same time it was the hardest because I had to telephone my parents and tell them what I had done. I hadn't told them what I planned on doing or where I was going before I left home. I couldn't because I knew they would have stopped me from enlisting. My sister Bertha had joined the Royal Canadian Air Force a year before, and her letters home indicated her life in the force was incredibly interesting. I wanted to experience the same.

Joining the RCAF-WD

I joined the Royal Canadian Air Force - Women's Division in Calgary, Alberta on October 23, 1942, immediately following my eighteenth birthday. The first assignment I received was to go for Basic Training in Toronto at the Manning Depot Training Centre, which would take about six months. As soon as I had completed my training I was transferred to Winnipeg, Manitoba to work in the accounts section for the RCAF - WD. It was interesting work but being somewhat lonely I didn't stay there very long. I asked to be posted in Calgary, Alberta where all my friends were. My request for transfer was granted and I was sent back to the Calgary area about six months later.

Logging Flights

I was sent to the #19 SFTS Service Line Training School for Pilots in Vulcan, Alberta. I worked as a secretary for Control Tower, Wing Commander Davenport. I had to log all the flights and had the responsibility of tracking every pilot's airtime. I used a call radio to track the boys and speak to them as they flew. The information had to be very accurate, because the pilots in training had to have a certain amount of hours before they could receive their wings. When a group completed their training we would have a big graduation parade on the base before they were shipped out by train. They never knew where they were going; just went wherever they were needed.

I enjoyed my work and life in the air force. I started as an Aircraft Woman and with a lot of hard work and training, I ended my time in the service as a Leading Air Craft Woman. I also had wonderful clothes to wear; this was a bonus, as our uniforms were very neat and sharp looking. They were made of blue serge wool with beautiful caps and a very nice gold insignia on the front, and gold buttons that made us look so good. We wore oxford shoes with heels, and a greatcoat that fit over the uniform in winter. Summer uniforms were very similar but were made of a lighter gabardine material. I was very proud to wear that uniform.

Practical Jokes

My sister Bertha was stationed near me for a time and we would often travel home on leave together. She was always a great practical joker and often got laughs at my expense. However, one day I got her back. We were going home for a visit on our weekend leave by train and as we sat chatting and watching the world go by, a very handsome air force officer was making his way along the isle of the train. As he passed our seats I got very daring and gave a low wolf whistle to which he spun around and looked directly at us. At this I turned to Bertha and said in a loud voice, "Shame on you! You know you are not allowed to make passes or whistle at an officer". Bertha was stunned to silence at my remark and cheekiness and later vowed to get even. The officer was very gracious; he just smiled and went on his way.

Skiing in Banff

We were allowed a pass to go off the base every second Saturday. A group of girls would go into a small township called Vulcan, Alberta. We had a lot of fun there just being with each other, listening to music, dancing and visiting. We also got to take trips to Banff whenever we had a 72-hour pass. In the winter we went skiing at Sunshine and Norquay ski resorts.

I met my first husband at the #19 SFTS Service Line Training School. He was Training Instructor Flight Lieutenant Wallace John Keane of the Royal Australian Air Force; an Aussie from Melbourne, Australia. A girlfriend and I played badminton on the base almost every night when we were not on duty. Wallace and his New Zealand mate Don also played regularly and we would chat during breaks. Eventually he asked me out on a date after which we started courting. We got along right from the start. I believe it was because we had the same interests; he enjoyed skiing, and he was all the more interesting as he was an Aussie.

Married In New York, USA

We were married on July 09, 1945 in New York, in a little church three months before we were discharged from the forces in Sept 08, 1945. We went to New York to be married because Wallace was supposed to be sent overseas soon and New York was close to Munction New Brunswick where he was stationed. We both had leave so I got two girlfriends and Wallace got two boys with him and we went to Winnipeg, Manitoba then to Montreal, Quebec, and on to New York. We all made this journey by train; the trip was a great experience in itself, one I won't forget. We were all young and I was on my way to become a bride.

25

It was a lovely wedding and we were able to have pictures taken that I sent home so I could in some way share this wonderful day with my family. Before my new husband could be shipped overseas to help continue the fight, the war came to an end so he shipped out for home instead. I was not able to join him at that time but only a short time later I sailed from Canada to join him in Australia on the 12th of October 1945. He met me in Brisbane when I arrived and from there we made our way to Melbourne where we set up the house that was our first home. We had two daughters, Gail in 1946 and Carol in 1950

My Homes in Australia

We lived in suburban Melbourne where Wallace was an accountant with the Mobil Oil Company and eventually built a very nice house in Balwyn where we lived for a number of years. Sadly after thirteen years we separated and subsequently divorced. I moved with my two girls to Shepparton in county Victoria, where I later met and eventually married my second husband, Bob Byham, a widower with four children and an engineer by profession. Both of my daughters lived with us so it was quite a houseful for a while. Gail was the first to leave when at seventeen she went to share a house with an elderly couple as a measure of her independence. Carol remained with us for a few more years until she left to become an exchange student in the Philippines. Bob and I divorced some years later and I decided I needed to go home to Canada for my first visit since I left in 1945,

Back home in Canada

When I did go back my first impression was; what a difference! Everything was changed. I went back to Vulcan, to see what it would look like now. If I was looking for change, I was not disappointed. There are a lot more people living there now, and they had cement sidewalks. When I was there during the war there were wooden sidewalks, we called them "duck walks". The biggest change for me was when I visited the old airplane hanger and found out it had been converted into a community hall. The visit brought back a lot of good memories.

I didn't recognize my younger brothers and sisters and the old houses in my hometown had somehow changed. My dad was gone too; he had passed away on July 14, 1972. I returned to Canada once again in 1995 for a Houle family reunion. I decided I would like to live in Alberta again and I did manage to stay for eighteen months, but the winter was too cold and so much snow, I found it hard to cope with climate and winter temperatures so I returned to Australia. I love Canada and a part of my heart will always be there but I found that when I was there I developed a longing for my adopted country and I became so lonely for family and friends in Australia and knew I just had to return.

I had a variety of jobs to make ends meet, and one that I recall with a lot of affection was as a cook in a snow lodge at Bulla in the Victorian Alps. It was very hard and demanding work but what little leisure time we had was just the best ski time. It was really great fun. We sure tamed that mountain!

My Family Today

Now in 2003, I am a pensioner and spend my time partly with Gail and her partner Peter on their small farm in Yarra Glen, Victoria and partly with Carol who now lives in Townsville in the north of sunny Queensland some three hours flying time away. Gail never had any children and is a great animal lover and caregiver. Carol had five children that have all left home and now she lives happily in the sunshine. Her son and one of her four daughters live nearby, whilst her youngest daughter lives in Albury, Victoria. None of these grandchildren are married. Carol's other two daughters both live in England. One, Michele has four children and is happily married and the other daughter Christine is getting married next year. All of Carol's children are very independent and are successful in their careers. I enjoy being a mother, grandmother and great-grandmother; I just wish I lived closer to all of my family.

I have enjoyed going back in time with my memories, realizing the opportunities and adventures I have had. My life's path has lead me a much different route, because of that impulsive decision to join the air force. It was a good decision!

PRIVATE GLADYS MARJORIE IRISH
A Woman of Strength and Determination

CWAC insignia

Photo courtesy of Gladys Irish (Sawchyn)
Gladys Irish in Uniform, 1942.

Carefree Days of Summer

My childhood happened so long ago; but it is something I can still recall as though it were yesterday. I spent those first golden years of my life on our family farm where I grew up with three of my two sisters and four brothers. My parents had settled down on a parcel of land that was three and one half miles from High Prairie, Alberta. It was a beautiful place to live, rolling hills dotted by forests, lakes and rivers and miles of prairie surrounded us. And it seems that the days were filled with sunshine, during all seasons. I especially love reminiscing about the long and carefree days of summer that filled my childhood. Some of the best times for me were when all of our family would go picking blue berries together. Berry picking was fun, at least for me, because it was a time when everyone got together to camp out, visit and just be with each other. We all knew that the purpose of the ventures into the bush was to gather the berries that would provide us with fruit throughout the winter, but more than that it was a time for the community to connect. It was especially good for the younger people and children because, like today, there is still nothing as important as seeing your family and friends.

Our Annual Berry Picking Camp Out

Many people joined together to go on these summer excursions, everyone from tiny babies to the Elders. I distinctly recall the Ferguson and LaRiviere families that were two of the large Métis families who would join in on the fun and work with us. This summer outing was considered our vacation because we would camp out overnight. Playing was our goal as children, but our parent's goal was to take home enough berries to preserve for the year. So my father, knowing us as he did, would pay my brothers, sisters and I, twenty-five cents to fill a large syrup pail full of blueberries. He would tell us with a smile on his face and a twinkle in his eye that we had to pick our quota before we could go and play. Filling our quota was never a problem, as we simply would pay the other children ten cents a bucketful of berries. In no time at all we could always get to go play sooner and be fifteen cents richer at the same time. My childhood was most certainly one of the experiences that forged me into the woman I am today. I now realize it was my parent's legacy, that was left to me, in turn, to pass on to others.

Traditional Métis Home Parties

As any farmer will know there is not much time for "good times" in the fall, it is mostly about work. Earning a living from the land could present more trials and tribulations than one could dream up but we always got through it very well. Our reward for the months of hard work came in the winter; once the toiling was done, that is. Once again we gathered, either as a family or as a larger group to do what we loved best, dance to the music of the fiddle. I loved the old time music and the way it inspired most of us to jig until the dust raised from beneath the floor boards. There were many times

Photo courtesy of Gladys Irish Sawchyn

Gladys and her brother, Alex Kieffer Irish, 1942. Gladys signed up with CWAC the following September.

when we would gather at someone's house, the women would all bring sandwiches and cakes and the men would bring their fiddles and guitars. We were "set" for the night. If there was any beer or moonshine brought to the parties, it was left outside for the men to go out to drink it. Hard liquor was very hard to come by; so it was always homemade. The children learned by having to dance with an older partner, that way we were taught the wonderful and exciting traditional Métis dances.

Signing Up on a Dare

I would often walk into town with my brothers after the day's work on the farm was finished. We would go to the Roxy Movie Theater in High Prairie. One summer day in 1942, after seeing a show, some friends and I went to the Spalding Hotel Restaurant for coffee. The first thing we noticed when we went in was some army recruiting officers who were sitting at a nearby table. My friends dared me to go over and sign up. I remember feeling excited and a little nervous at the idea but being one who never turned down a dare, I took them up on it. On that first day of September, in 1942 as a young girl of seventeen, I boldly walked across the restaurant floor, went over to the Recruiting Officers and gave them my name and address, lying through my teeth, I declared that I was 18 years of age; in that way I signed on to become a member of the Canadian Women's Army Corps.

Aside from being a feisty girl who couldn't turn down a dare, I had other reasons for signing up. This was soon after the "hungry 30's"; money was scarce, so all of the young people were joining up. It offered many opportunities to work at a job that would actually pay 65 cents per day, and I would be able to travel a bit. I had joined up with the Canadian Women's Army Corps - a division of the regular Canadian Army. By signing on, I had joined with thousands of other women across Canada who were being recruited to replace men in non-combat duty. The women working on the home front freed up the soldiers who went over-seas for service on the front lines with the Allied force in Europe.

The New Recruit

Shortly after signing on to be a new recruit, my parents came to give me a train ticket. The army had sent it to me by mail. The idea of leaving my home and family was scary because I had never been on my own before. The train ride Edmonton, Alberta was a new experience as was my first sight of the city. I remember, much to my relief, there was some one who had been sent to meet at the train station, and took me off to the Prince of Wales Armouries. Here I was assigned a room in the barracks, went for a medical to determine my fitness for service and received my regimental number W13496 and uniforms. The first uniform I received was a nice medium to dark brown coloured winter suit, with a tunic jacket and a straight skirt. The gold buttons had the crest of CWAC on them, our hats had a hardtop and peak, and they too had the CWAC crest on the front of it. Our shoes were nice soft brown leather oxfords with a one and a half inch heel. These shoes just didn't seem to ever wear out. I believe they were the best shoes I had ever worn. Later on we received the overcoats in the same colour, but in a heavier material. I believe they were wool. In the spring we received our summer uniforms, the same style but in a lighter weight and colour of material. I felt very proud and important to wear the uniform that told anyone at a glance that I was a woman serving her country. I am still proud of it today.

Basic Training

After all these necessary arrangements were made, I was sent to Vermillion, Alberta to complete three months of basic training. I thought life on the farm was hard, but I can honestly say I never had to punish my body by farm work in the way I had to as I went through the rigorous drills that was basic training. With the training behind me I was then transferred to Calgary where I remained for the next three and one half years. I wanted to go overseas, but when I was scheduled to go I inadvertently let my parents know and they contacted my commanding officer and reported that I was 17 years of age; as a result my application was denied. This meant I would remain in Canada on the home front. I was definitely disappointed, but I did not let my disappointment stop me from giving my best to the job I had signed on to do.

My New Life

At first I was a very lonely and homesick, but after a while I got used to living away from home. As a young woman I was a person who was eager to explore new ideas, adventures and especially to meet new people. It was not difficult for me, thanks to my parents and my great childhood, I met a lot of very interesting people from all over Canada. It was good to be with people who were like me in so many ways. We liked to get together to visit and share our own life stories with each other. In this way we all got over our sense of loneliness in a really short time.

Christmas at Home

I will never forget the first time I got leave to go home for Christmas, I was happy then that I had to remain in Canada because by this time I was aware of the horrendous ordeals other Canadians who were serving overseas, were going through. I realized the excruciating pain they endured, a result of war and loneliness, could not be even temporarily relieved by seeing family and friends at Christmas time. I was grateful that I was given a four-day leave to go visit with those I loved the most. I went home by train as they were running every day. Everyone was there to meet me and I stepped off the train into a group of people that I loved so much. I remember how the many faces there registered the same pride, excitement and love I was feeling. It was a long ride back, but was worth every minute and every mile because I was one of the few solders who was able to see their family at Christmas time.

Double Check The Guns and Ammunition

My first job was working in the kitchen after I joined the army. The work was nothing new and a little on the hum drum side, but I did it willingly as it was work that was necessary to the well being of the army. Later on I worked for the Royal Canadian Ordinance Corp in Calgary Alberta. It was like a clothing store, we fitted and gave the soldiers their new uniforms and personal items. Work life here was more interesting as we were taught new things. We had to learn how to assemble parcel packages that contained guns, ammunition and other smaller necessary equipment that would be sent to our solders overseas. We were kept very busy and we were always under supervision. We were told what to do all of the time; this was because packaging parcels were very important, lives depended on it. This work required a lot of time and people so we were housed in Sarcee Barracks. The barracks were great long houses that could accommodate sixty to eighty women in one hut.

The Camaraderie of Army Life

Life in the army wasn't all drudgery and hard work. There was also some time for a little fun and relaxation. I enjoyed the new clubroom that was built in Calgary at the women's auxiliary to the CWAC. I spent some of my time playing card games, darts and visiting with my comrades. Some days we would walk across the compound and go to the Salvation Army Hall, the "Sally Anne" as we affectionately called it. We could use their

Newspaper clipping courtesy of Gladys Irish (Sawchyn)

Above: This newspaper clipping shows the 'new club room' that Gladys mentions in her story under 'The Camaraderie of Army Life'. Gladys is in the top left corner of the photo that was taken in 1942.

library and write letters home or to the soldiers overseas, even if we didn't know the soldiers we would write to them as pen pals. In my free time I did what I liked doing the most, visiting with and talking to my buddies. I was not sport minded, so I never played ball or went bicycle or horse back riding like some of the other girls did.

The Rainbow Ballroom

I especially enjoyed the times we were allowed to go to into town to see a show and maybe go to the pubs once a month on paydays. I can remember attending the dances that were held in Calgary. I would dance with old friends I knew from home, and the new friends that I had made. I was not afraid to show off my talent in this area. Everyone I knew agreed by encouraging me to dance at every opportunity. I wasn't by any means the only good dancer back then; there were plenty of others who knew so many different kinds of steps like the two steps, jitterbugs, and waltzes. I remember us all dancing up a storm at the Rainbow Ballroom in Calgary. The entertainment was very good for the soldiers; I think like myself, many others lived with a lot of the stress that comes from serving during wartime, even on the home front. There were other activities and events arranged for us as well that I for one most certainly enjoyed. For example, there were different times when a bunch of us girls would take a bus to Banff and spend the day touring together. I am now happy and proud that I was a part of it all. The army was very good to me; I enjoyed the work I did and the people I worked with.

No Discrimination

There was another aspect of service life that was good; no discrimination! At least none that I was aware of, in the army everyone was treated as equals within the ranks. We worked hard together as a team and everybody just had a good time. Everyone was simply called by his or her last names. Our superiors treated us well too, everyone mingled except the officers. We weren't allowed to mix with them, but they too were friendly, and treated us with respect at all times.

We Were Meant to Be

I had my share of boyfriends and short-lived romances in the army, but the relationships never really got a chance to grow as the guy always got shipped overseas or was stationed some place else. That was until I met a friend from back home, his name was Matt Sawchyn. It was incredibly wonderful to go out with him; we had so much in common, so much to talk to each other about. We would talk about the times he and his family used to go picking berries with mine. Matt and I would go see a show then he would always walk me home afterwards.

Far too soon he received his orders for overseas duties. As soon as he went overseas I wrote to him, as often as possible, but I lost contact with him. This caused me some moments of distress but I continued on with my life in the army in much the same way as it had been before he had come into my life.

Photo courtesy of Gladys Irish Sawchyn

Above: This is a copy of Gladys Irish Sawchyn's
Discharge Certificate from Active Duty with the
Canadian Army dated October 23, 1945.

The Love of My Life

The great day finally came; the war was over! I received the Canadian
Volunteer Service Medal and was discharged on Oct 23, 1945. I returned
home to High Prairie. I continued my ongoing love affair with dancing; I
still knew the Red River jig and Highland fling that I was taught as a child
in my Métis community. One night soon after I got home, I went to a
dance in the High Prairie Red Barn, and lo and behold there he was! I
couldn't believe my eyes, but I was able to believe my heart as my hand-

some Mathew crossed the dance floor with a smile on his face to ask me to dance. The rest is history. We were married April 23, 1946. We had 5 children, 3 girls and 2 boys, 8 grandchildren and 3 great-grandchildren. Matt passed away in the fall of '95. I now live in Grande Prairie, Alberta with my daughter Christine Bugar and her husband and family. Once again I have my friends, family and the community I now live in to support and love me. Today I am recognized as an Elder, by a wonderful women's organization called the Institute for the Advancement of Aboriginal Women. I participate in a senior's group three times per week.

Now as I look back I am very happy that I joined the army. It was a very positive experience, I gained more self-confidence and I am very proud to know I served my country.

FIGHTER CONTROL OPERATOR
THERESA LOYIE

The Spirit of Adventure

RCAF insignia

Photo courtesy of Theresa Anderson

Theresa Anderson in her RCAF -
Airwomen's Division uniform, 1952.

My Young Life

When I was born 0n May 22 of 1932, so was my spirit of adventure. My parent's were Henry and Clara Loyie née Cunningham. We lived on my uncle Ed's farm in Calahoo, Alberta. I was raised there with my three sisters and two brothers until I was thirteen years old. During this time I attended the Granger School, two miles north of Calahoo. This meant we had to walk three miles one way to get to school. We would cut across fields so we could meet with our cousins and walk the rest of the way with them. Sometimes getting to school was a challenge, but I remember that it was also a good time in my life, the challenges just made it more interesting.

Soon after this time our family experienced a tragic loss when our father passed away from heart disease. This meant our family had to make changes in our way of life, so my mother decided to move her family to Rivie re Qui Barre, Alberta where she was able to rent a house from Mrs. Theobald Majeau. The house was a closer walk to the school and this would enable her to better provide for her family, as there would be more resources available. Mother understood that not only must she provide for her children in terms of food, clothing and shelter, but that she must also provide us with the knowledge and skills that would help us to further develop a pride in our Métis culture and Aboriginal heritage. As a result she taught us all how to do the traditional Métis dances at a very early age. We learned many dances that included: "the Red River Jig, Drops of Brandy, Reel of Eight, the Chicken Dance and the Duck Dance". I remember my uncle Frank Loyie, my father's youngest brother, being part of these activities and it still delights me to recall the many happy hours he would spend dancing the Red River Jig with me.

After completing grade eight we had to move again so I could continue with my high school education. We moved right into Calahoo and I was able to start school there and continued until I finished grade eleven.

Education was something that was really important to me and I wanted to get my grade twelve. I wasn't able to do this in Calahoo, as they did not teach grade twelve at the high school there so I had to move yet again. This time the move meant leaving my home and family to go live with my aunt, Alice Cunningham, in St. Albert, Alberta.

Looking back I know without a doubt it was all worth the hard work and loneliness I endured during that period in my life. I take pride in the fact that I was among the first group to graduate from St. Albert High School in 1952. I now realize this was quite an accomplishment at that time for a Métis person, especially a female to earn a high school diploma. I believe there were three of us Métis students from St Albert, to do this in the early 1950's.

My Curiosity About a Bigger World

When I turned 20 years old, my spirit of adventure began to stir to such a degree that I could no longer ignore it. I realized I had achieved all of the educational goals I had aimed for and now I needed more of a challenge. I decided that I had to do something different; it was time to take another step on my life's journey to find more adventures, and at the same time satisfy my curiosity about the bigger world. I just knew I wanted to be a part of it all and maybe at the same time I could continue to pursue my dream of attaining a higher level of education.

Signed Up on The Spot

So I determinedly set out to explore the world and what opportunities awaited me. I had heard about the Royal Canadian Air Force (RCAF) recruiting office on Kingsway Avenue in Edmonton, Alberta and decided I would go there. Once inside I knew I had found what I was looking for. Without any hesitation, on July 17, 1952 I signed up on the spot to become the newest member of the RCAF-Airwomen's Division. I have never regretted the decision I made on what I now consider to be one of the most fateful days of my life.

Soon after I signed up I was sent to the Air Force Base in Edmonton where I underwent a medical examination, that I readily passed, I was then issued my uniforms and was assigned my service number 209512W. Immediately after these exercises were completed, I found I would be travelling to Eastern Canada. They sent me off to St Jean, Quebec for eight weeks of basic training. The trip east was both scary and exciting for me at the same time. I can remember feeling a little lonesome at first but I soon got over it. There was no looking back as far as I was concerned, it was what I wanted to do. I wanted to see what the rest of the world was like. My feelings turned into excitement because at last I was really on my own and going on a big adventure.

FCO#96

REAR ROW - J Quinn, JT Loyie, DJ Leason, JE Fullerton, VM Hlohovosky.
CENTRE ROW - IB Trainor, G Shiel, JED MacNiel, G Lindgaard, MK Williams, MD McCarthy.
FRONT ROW - EM Short, HM Jordan, SE Wilson, MA Shea, EN Bertrand.

The Scope Dope

The train trip itself turned out to be a great experience because I met another girl from Ardrosan, Alberta, named Lynn Holseth. We made friends right from the start and we were lucky enough to become roommates once we arrived at our destination.

Once my basic training was completed I was sent to trade training in Clinton, Ontario for a period of three months. When I got there I was intrigued to find out I would be living with the rest of my unit in Quonset huts. Trades training meant I had to begin taking instructions that would prepare me to become a Fighter Control Operator, which included training to work with Radar, the nickname given to this particular position was "Scope Dope". I had to give information to the plotting tables and weather reporters in Falconbridge, Ontario. Soon after this phase of training was completed I earned the position of Fighter Control Operator (FCO - fighter cop). The most exciting part of the training for me, was working with CF-100 airplanes when they engaged in mock fighter exercises. I loved watching the death defying manoeuvres those brave young men made. I knew how dangerous it was. This was crucial information that we collected and then sent on to North Bay and Montreal to be analyzed in detail. The exercises were held on a regular basis because they still had to be prepared in case a war broke out again.

The Pine Tree Line

The area we were responsible for was to provide cover for the Pine Tree Line, the DEW line was farther north of the Pine Tree Line and both were taken care of in a similar fashion that involved manning radar bases. From what I remember, the construction of the Pine Tree Line started out as a joint venture between the Royal Canadian Air force and the American Air Force early in the 1950's. The line started in St. Margarite, New Brunswick right into the interior of BC. The purpose of this project was to construct strategically located radar stations that were built and designed as the primary line of air defence warning to counter the Soviet air threat against North America. The threat was real so this is where our unit came in; it was up to us to man the stations.

The Snack Bar

There was a lot of hard work in the RCAF, but there was a lot of fun too. I was not by any means a sports person but I certainly enjoyed participating as a dedicated fan in the events that were held. There were other social activities provided by the base and being a gregarious person by nature, I took advantage of the opportunities to socialize and have fun. I spent much of my free time in the Recreation Centre at the snack bar. Here we could get our hair done, go bowling, play basket ball, or see a show. The snack bar was equipped with a jukebox and I spent many pleasant hours there, as I loved to dance. I believe we had so many social activities provided for us because we all were young then and needed to have something to occupy our free time to make sure that we stayed well behaved.

Sheet Exchange Duty

I had other duties to perform; one of them included sheet exchange. This meant I was responsible for gathering the soiled sheets, take them to the laundry in a truck that was usually driven by a male driver and collect fresh sheets that I was responsible for returning to the woman's barracks. One day, just before Christmas, a new transport driver came to pick up the laundry and me. He was a very attractive young man, but I managed to keep my thoughts to myself as we went in to the barracks to get the sheet bins. Upon entering I hollered, as I had been trained to: " Man in Barracks". The good-looking driver got a little upset about my shouted warning and said, "What did you do that for?" I simply ignored him and just continued to lead him around the barracks to gather the bins, loaded them up and got into the truck with him to go get the fresh sheets. When we returned, I yelled out the same thing and again he got upset, this time I told him I was just doing my job.

I later learned that a fire inspector, Harvey, had told this new driver that when they would inspect the barracks unexpectedly he got to see the girls in different stages of undress. It seemed as though our new driver was now looking forward to the same experience and was a little bit put out because my warning denied him of it. I later found out the new transport driver was a LAC Stuart Anderson (Leading Air Craftsman) everyone called "Andy". I saw him around the place now and again and I tried not to give it too much thought. Then on the evening of my 22nd birthday in May, I was at the snack bar in the recreation centre waiting with friends to go out and see a show when Andy unexpectedly arrived. When my friends told Andy it was my birthday he asked "How many years?" When he got the answer, he promptly flipped me over his knee and gave me 23 paddles, one for each year and one for good luck. To this day I still think Andy must have liked the feel of my firm bottom because he sure came around after that, and I really didn't do too much to discourage the attention he was giving me.

Riding In a Canvas Covered Transport Truck

Andy started to do special things for me, such as making sure I got to ride up front of the canvas covered truck that he drove to transport the women from Sudbury into Falconbridge where we worked each day. He was also there to drive us home after work each evening. This was a sixteen-mile trip and it didn't matter what the weather was like, we had to go to work anyway. When it was 40 below Fahrenheit, it got pretty cold in the back with no heat and only a canvas cover on the box of the 2 1/2-ton transport truck. The only comfort provided back there was just seats on either side and down the middle. To add to the misery, if the driver was not a good one, the riders would end up all squashed together or on the floor. So I did not complain when I was invited to sit in the front cab, and besides, I got to be with Andy.

The Proposal, and Wedding Day Surprise

On one of these trips, with just Andy and myself up in the front, he asked me to marry him. I was thrilled, excited and honoured, but I said no. Andy wasn't one to give up on anything he wanted, he persisted by coming around often enough to convince me I couldn't live without him. I finally said yes and after getting permission from the Queen, we were married in Garson Mines, Ontario, on November 13,1954. I will never forget the wedding surprise Andy had planned for our special day. Without me knowing, he managed to sneak my mother to Capreoal, Ontario, all the way from Calahoo, Alberta, so she could be there for our wedding day. He arranged the train trip east for her so she would arrive just in time for the wedding. As Andy had never met my mother, he told her to look for a fellow in uniform. Andy was standing on the train station platform in Capreoal waiting for her train to arrive, when much to his dismay, a train from the east came in loaded with men all in uniform. He had some pretty tense moments sweating it out for a while, wondering how his future mother-in-law would ever pick him out in that group.

Photo courtesy of Theresa Anderson

Theresa Loyie and Stuart (Andy) Anderson on their Wedding Day.

Lucky for Andy they had all left minutes before mother arrived on the train from the west. The Catholic priest performed the wedding service in the church at Garson Mines. The reception was held in the lounge in the Mess Hall Building, with 40 or so guests from the base.

Honourable Discharge

I stayed in the RCAF until I took my discharge July 16, 1955 because my term was up and I had become pregnant. In those days if you were pregnant you had to leave the forces. I remember there were times when a girl would be in tears, pack her bags and leave with no explanation. Andy stayed in the service until he retired, therefore, so did I as his wife. In this way I did get to travel and live in other countries. It was great, I had my husband and children by my side, I found the adventures I was looking for and the adventure still continues. We have six children and ten grandchildren and now that Andy has retired we permanently live in Edmonton, Alberta and will be celebrating our 50th wedding anniversary in 2004.

Remaining Active

From my lifetime of living this great adventure I learned so much, it was an amazing experience that gave me the self - confidence, education and training that I have been able to use throughout my life. It also helped me be a successful Air Force wife. Another bonus from my time of service is that I made friendships that have lasted until today. I continue to enjoy remaining an active member of the FCO's. I never miss the reunions we have, the most recent ones have been in Red Deer, Lethbridge, and Summerside, PEI and the ex-RCAF Women's Association of Alberta is having their reunion this year in Edmonton. I am looking forward to the reunion this year from June 5 to 8/ 2003. I am also actively involved in the organization of it. Many of my friends from different bases that I was stationed at have called me about it. It is still exciting to be a part of it all;

45

especially when one of my former roommates Iline Short from Newfoundland called me to say she would soon be seeing me.

Retirement

Andy and I have retired in Edmonton, Alberta with our children and grandchildren around us and I still love to dance. I stay involved in a tap dance group, which includes my daughter Holly Hardeman; we have performed at the Myer Horowitz Theatre, Jubilee Auditorium, Winspear Theatre and the Banff School of Fine Arts. My two granddaughters also dance with us at the same studio. We have a four-year-old granddaughter that dances in Spruce Grove, Alberta. I guess she takes after her grandmother. We still live a very happy and fulfilling life together.

AIR WOMAN
MARGUERITE ST. GERMAINE

A Remarkable Journey

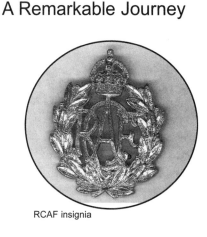

RCAF insignia

Photo courtesy of Marguerite St. Germaine
Marguerite St. Germaine, 1943.

Born in the snow storm of 1922

It snowed heavily on the day I was born, August 28th 1922. My father kept records of unusual weather and his records show that in the Peace River Valley it had snowed about three feet. Our family lived in Grayling Creek at the time where my parents homesteaded. I lived with them until I reached the age of eighteen and the eleventh grade in 1940. I then moved to McLennan where I found work with a family who ran a boarding house. I was able to work in the boarding house restaurant for $25.00 a month. My wages enabled me to pay for room and board. In this way I was able to finish high school.

Joining up

I enjoyed living in McLennan, Alberta, but I knew there was more out there for me to see and do. Like any other Canadian at the time I was aware that we were at war with Germany. I knew that many of our men and women were fighting daily on the European front to keep those of us at home safe. As a fiercely patriotic Canadian I wanted to do my part to help protect my country, so I decided to join up I had to be in

Edmonton, Alberta for Nov 22nd 1942 to be sworn in with the Royal Canadian Air Force (RCAF) Women's Division. I joined up because, first of all I was patriotic, and secondly I had been born with the spirit of an explorer, I knew joining up would allow me to travel the great distances I had always dreamed of. Enlisting turned out to be one of the greatest things I have ever done. It gave me the chance to get out of Northern Alberta, see some of the world, go on a great adventure to who knows where and have the experience of a lifetime.

Basic Training

The new experience started when I boarded the train, as ordered, and left the North for Edmonton. I will never forget that trip. It was wonderful, exciting and scary all at the same time. I had never been so far from home before. I was amazed at all the new exciting sounds, smells, sights and the new people that I was introduced to. My girlfriend, Marie Boulaine from St Paul, Alberta and I had agreed to meet in Edmonton. It turned out that she didn't show up until December. When she did arrive we were sent by train to Ontario. The train had five coaches full of girls from the west who, like Marie and I, were all being transported to Rockcliff Ontario Training Centre for basic training. This made for an interesting and exciting trip for us all as most of the girls, not unlike my friend and I, had never been more than a few miles away from home. Our similar backgrounds and the situation the world was in at the time

Photos courtesy of Marguerite St. Germaine

Top Left: Marguerite and friend (Ross Brele) the day she enlisted November 11,1942.
Top Right: Marguerite working as a 'steno' with a manual typewriter in 1942.

seemed to bind us all together in a way that could probably never happen under different circumstances. We shared many stories and taught each other new dances and songs; in this way we formed a sisterhood that helped define who we were and what we were doing. It made us a unique group in Canadian history. I made myself very clear to the recruiters when I signed up that I was not interested in joining up to become a dishwasher. They knew that I wanted to work in the office. As a result of my request I was able to attend night school for 4 hours every evening after putting in my required days work. I worked hard during the next six-months to complete a crash course to train as a steno. I was good at it and excelled in typing and shorthand. I could type 65 to 75 words per minute on a manual typewriter. I achieved this because of my determination and the support of the best teacher in the world.

I did not like my first few months in Rockcliff, but I felt better after I got a proper fitting uniform and was transferred to Toronto for three weeks as a clerk general. I was stationed in Arnprior, Ontario # 3 FIS. I was the 65th Airwoman. I enjoyed my job immensely as a flight time - keeper. I had the responsibility of keeping absolutely accurate records of flying hours for the pilots in training, because they needed 400 hours of flying time to graduate. To ensure the records were accurate, the trainer would come into the administration office where I worked, to sign my daily logbook. I also worked in the Administration Building in the signals department. I worked both these jobs until I was transferred to the Women's Department offices that summer. I look back on that period of my life as a transforming one because I gained so much experience and at the same time achieved a higher level of education. It seemed like I had become a new person, so much so that it would be hard to recognize me as the same girl who had left Northern Alberta such a short time ago.

History in the Making

As that wonderful summer saw its completion so did my job in Rockcliff. I was then stationed for a while in Montreal, Quebec. I remained there until June of 1943 when I was transferred to Ottawa, Ontario. I was so amazed and excited to be stationed there, in the capital city of Canada! More importantly, I was assigned to work in the heart of our political focal point, right in the buildings of Parliament. I felt significant, special, and extremely proud because I had earned the right to serve there, being the only one chosen for this assignment from my department because I had a clean discipline sheet. My duties there were spent working for the finance office throughout the summer of 1944. I saw many members of our elected leadership as a part of my position. This included seeing Mackenzie King, the Prime Minister of Canada, almost every day for four months.

A lot of people from all the other Canadian armed forces worked in the Parliament Buildings as well. This included many girls from different countries such as New Zealand and Australia. It was quite a happy experience in a time of sadness. I made a lot of new friends, especially with some of the girls from the Navy who were stationed at Bytown (Old Ottawa) and went to visit with them as often as I was able. Being surrounded by a place where so many decisions were being made on behalf of the Canadian citizens helped me to always strive for excellence in my work, but at the same time my sense of adventure and fun flourished within me. I was always a daredevil and I recall with great delight how I nose saluted a rookie RCMP in Ottawa one day. I remember he was so shocked that he didn't know what to do, so he ignored me and pretended not to notice me. What made this time for me an even more exciting experience was when I attended sessions in Parliament I got to see history in the making. The memory of that summer remains clearly with me to this day.

No Overseas Service for Me

About this time I started thinking of applying for overseas service, when my brother, Staff Sergeant Joseph St. Germaine, called me and said not to come over to England. He was in Europe at the time and suggested I see Canada first. He said I had a wonderful opportunity to do so and should take advantage of it. He also said he did not want me to go overseas because the fighting there was bad with a lot of bombing taking place at the time. I listened to his advice and did not apply for overseas duties. As a result, one of

Above: Marguerite St. Germaine's brother Staff Sergeant Joseph St. Germaine - killed in action Dec 14, 1944.

my friends Molly Wallsmith from Notikewin, Alberta took my place and she went off to England. She was happy to go because she had a boyfriend stationed there. I am glad I took my brother's advice and remained in Canada but it still hurts to say I was never to see my brother again. He was killed in action in the water on Dec 14, 1944 at the Riviglio Canal and he is buried in Ravenna, Italy. My greatest wish now is to go there to visit his grave.

New Year's Eve in Times Square

Although there was a lot of hard work, grief, and loss, there were also good times. Throughout it all I made lifelong friends that I still write to today. I fondly remember the wonderful days when we would often get together to take bicycle tours through Montreal and the Ottawa Valley. There were times we even travelled to New York and one time in particular that I remember well was in 1944 when we all went to Times Square to celebrate New Year's Eve together. On another trip to New York we met and made friends with some black people along the way and ended up spending a part of our day with them, which made our trip more delightful. They liked Canadians, and took us to Harlem for their Easter Parade, their costumes were very colourful, and the children were so cute. All of my friends were "white" and at that time none of us realized that as black people they were used to being treated "differently". They enjoyed the day as well because of the way we accepted them as simply a group of people, not unlike ourselves. It never occurred to our group to act any differently. I would suppose this was because we never had to deal with racial issues in the Armed Forces. My philosophy is "what does the difference in colour mean anyway". I believe we all had this attitude if anyone ever thought of it. Furthermore, it didn't matter to any of us; we were all there as a team with an important job to do. I now realize that it was because of this philosophy and sense of oneness that I never experienced any oppression from being Aboriginal and a woman as well.

Favourite Pastimes

Music and dancing had been a part of my childhood and throughout my life. I have continued to love them both. In the armed forces listening to music and going to dances became some of my favourite pastimes. A friend and I were singing in the canteen one evening and a WD Officer came over and asked us to sing with a dance band, that was great fun for one summer. I had the opportunity to enter a dance marathon and I signed up with a partner who loved to dance as much as I did. We danced for 48 hours, and ended up taking second place! There were many times when a bus would pick up the girls and we would go to the Petawawa Army Base for more dancing. It seemed as though there was always a sea of men there. They were wall-to-wall. All of the girls had a dance card and as soon as we entered the dancehall, the soldiers would line up to sign our cards as quickly as they could as they overwhelmingly outnumbered us. There were so many soldiers there you could only dance once with each man in one evening. This stood even if you were attracted to one special guy or found one that turned out to be a great dancer.

Ottawa Civic Hospital

I also enjoyed playing fastball, I used to play on a team back home. We played on an excellent girls team who were terrific ball players. We were able to keep up our skills with the game by practicing with the airmen. The games were exciting and we always looked forward to them as everyone enjoyed the good-natured rivalry. I particularly remember one game with good reason. When I was playing on third base, I didn't see the ball that an air service man threw in my direction. It hit me smack on the nose and I was taken off the field and straight to the Ottawa Civic Hospital where they discovered my nose was badly broken. When they took me into the hospital I remember I was so scared, mainly because while I lay there on a stretcher, much to my chagrin, I saw a whole bunch of "stiffs" in the hallway. I later learned they had me down by the morgue. I didn't know why and I didn't know what was going on. I just know I was scared and confused.

All I could remember seeing before they finally put me out was the doctor who attended me being a weird looking little old man with a beard. While I was out they packed my nose with yards and yards of gauze, which was really uncomfortable. After a few days had passed and I had healed a bit, I found I had to take the gauze out myself. When I couldn't dislodge it, a nurse hit me on the back and it popped out. I almost passed out from the pain. I spent eleven days in the hospital until someone made a slip-up and I was released without notice to my superiors. Because of this I had no one from the base to pick me up. I walked the streets until I found a union bus to take me to the train station. I wasn't afraid because I knew the Arnprior van would be there to pick up passengers when I got off the train at the base. When I arrived the driver was very apologetic for not picking me up at the hospital, but due to the slip-up he had no way of knowing that I had been released.

The Repatriation Department

After all this I was transferred once again, to spend some of my time in the service at Arnprior Flight Engineering School. I remained there until October 1944 when I was transferred to Lychene Repatriation with the Air force Repatriation Department for the prisoners of war. It was here that the returning Commissioned Officers and Airmen from Europe first arrived. I now found myself working for the Repat - Depot in the Department of Pay and Accounts. I used to type thousands of pages that showed the amount of money the returning airmen were to receive.

The Repatriation Department was set up specifically to receive them. The first group to arrive was 2,500 airmen; some came from hospitals in England and others from prisoner of war camps and had been starved for years. These were so thin, sick, and depressed and in a very sorry state when they returned. Our hearts went out to them as we all wanted to help them ease the pain and memories that had been inflicted on them by the horrors they had endured fighting for our people.

We decided one good way to start with their healing process was to make a party just for them. So one evening we all got together to do just that. Our Wing Commander Daws, who came from the Dawes Family, owned a brewery. The Dawes Brewery generously donated all the beer anyone wanted to drink in aide of the returning prisoners of war. Some of the girls put on civilian clothes and served them hors d´oeuvres, sandwiches, and drinks. The returning airmen were in such poor physical shape that they soon became sick and some were crying. It turned out that this was not such a good idea. In fact, it was a heart wrenching experience for me. I know Canada treated their prisoners of war a lot better then the enemy treated ours. I still think of all those men and hope they managed to find some sort of peace and happiness.

Victory in Europe

I will never forget the day we finally got to celebrate our Victory in Europe (VE Day). It just happened that on that particular day, my girlfriend Irene Jones and I went to Montreal to see a Gershwin Play called "Rhapsody in Blue". When we came out of the theatre at four o'clock in the afternoon we didn't know what was going on. To our amazement we saw cars and taxis making an incredible racket by slowly driving down the streets honking their horns. Airplanes were dropping leaflets, there was paper flying everywhere from the sky and the tall buildings. The businesses had come to a halt; all of the streetcars and trains weren't running, we couldn't get a train back to the base but somehow we managed to stop a taxicab and jumped in as quickly as possible. We did not want to risk being late and written up as AWOL. Just as I jumped into the taxi, someone grabbed my hat. This gave me cause for worry because this now meant I was in public and out of uniform, but no one seemed to care. The people were wild and I was afraid they were going to strip our uniforms off of us for their souvenirs. We met the Police and when they didn't even ask me where my hat was, as they most certainly would have at any other time, it became clear to me that this was an indication of the celebratory mindset of the nation. It was made even clearer when after the 10-mile ride back to Lachine; the Taxi driver didn't charge us for the ride. He just gave us a wave and said, "It's over now, and you have done your job"!

When we got to the base there were people running around everywhere. Both the Officer's and Sergeant's Mess Halls were opened; they had a band playing and people were singing. We joined some of the people doing the Congo Line and as one passed by the bar someone would put a drink in your hand. The band played all night long. It was the happiest and best time I have ever seen while in the service. It was so great; I love to relive it often in my memory and share the memories. The sacrifices that were made by so many people and the way we celebrated our victory should never be forgotten.

Married in March of '46

During my time in the service I had a lot of dates and had a lot of fun, but I found it was wise to never get too serious with a guy, because as soon as I started to get to know one it seemed they were always being shipped overseas. Then I met a fellow towards the end of the war, who was stationed at my base. I had just been offered the chance to go to the Pacific, but I turned it down because of him. This fellow turned out to be my first husband Bernard (Blondie) Hallday who was stationed in the RCAF in Kinston, Ontario. He was in the same department as I was. We were married in March of 46, while we were still in uniform. We both received Honourable Discharges in April 1946. After being discharged

Photo courtesy of Marguerite St. Bermaine
Marguerite and her first husband
Bernard (Blondin) Hallday, 1946.

we moved on to Kingston Ontario. The surrounding countryside was very beautiful, with many lakes and excellent fishing, but I didn't like the weather. I especially did not like the terrible thunderstorms and the occasional tornado.

One day we went for a drive to the Six Nations Indian Reserve. The Indian Reserve was a farming community with a lot of nice big farms. They were wonderful farmers and it didn't look any different than any of the other places around there. The people from town spoke highly of the Indian farmers, and said they grew the best corn in the world. We were able to settle down there and continued to live in Ontario for a period of five and half years, during which time we had three children. After that time passed, I took the children and moved back to good old Alberta.

My Friend - The Most Wonderful Man in the World

I now live in Grande Prairie, Alberta with my second husband Phillip Plante. He is a wonderful man, who made my children fall in love with him first, before he asked me out. It was my mother who initially convinced me to go dancing with him. I hadn't danced for so long that it didn't take very much coaxing to convince me. He was a great dancer and danced right into my heart. Phil said the children and I fit into his life and his extended family so well that he knew we were meant to be together. We will be celebrating our forty-fifth anniversary this September 2003. We moved to Grande Prairie in 1962 where Phil worked for the Canadian Freightways and I worked for the Grande Prairie Municipal Hospital for twelve years as a medical records technician. Then Phil and I worked for the mentally challenged adults in Grande Prairie. We have three children. Earl, Donald, and Sharon Halladay. When we were first married, Phil and I discussed adoption with the children and they said, " It doesn't take a piece of paper to make you our Dad". We have nine grandchildren and ten great grandchildren. In my retirement years, I enjoy our family, as they have always been very important to me. I still love to read and I have a free membership to the Grande Prairie Library.

I am not physically active now but I still support my community by playing Bingo. I reminisce a lot with Phil and the children. I believe the RCAF gave me the experience, advantage, and education of a lifetime while helping to shape the person I am. I, Marge Plante, have lived a great life!

SERGEANT DOROTHY BELLEROSE
A Proud Canadian Metis Woman

CWAC insignia

Photo Courtesy of Dorothy Chartrand (Bellerose)

Dorothy Bellerose in 1945 on her wedding day.

My Metis Family

On Aug 15, 1918 I was born in St. Albert, Alberta of Métis parents, Pierre and Justine Bellerose, née Beaudry. They lived on farmland obtained through Métis Scrip by my grandfather Octave Bellerose in 1886. My parents were considered to be successful farmers in the area as they were able to make a good living for our family. There were thirteen children in all, seven daughters and six sons. I loved having so many brothers and sisters in my family; having them meant I was never lonely and always had a friend to play with. It also meant that there were many others to share the countless chores that came from operating a farm.

We were all taught how to run a farm early in life, and as farming is labour intensive, we also learned to work hard. My father owned another farm in Colinton, near Athabasca, at the same time so it was left up to my older brother and sister to work on that one. I lived with them for two years while I went to school.

The Old St. Albert School

I received most of my early education in the Guilbault School near the farm in St, Albert. This school was an old four-room schoolhouse up on the hill - I believe it was demolished around 1968. While I lived in Colinton I completed grade eleven there. I rode my horse to school every day for the whole two years, a memorable experience to say the least. In1936 I went back to St Albert to complete grade twelve. We didn't have a regular high school in St Albert at that time, so the grade ten, eleven and twelve students had to use the basement, which consisted of a room with two small windows. I recall it had a small science laboratory on one end located right next to a wood-burning furnace. We only had one teacher so sixteen of us students were all taught together down there.

I continued my education at St Mary's High School in Edmonton where I lived with some friends of my family for two years. In that time I studied for and received my matriculation diploma and a one-year commercial business course. I learned shorthand, typing, bookkeeping, accounting, penmanship, rapid math calculations, and business practices. Looking back I now realize this was quite an accomplishment for a Métis woman of that time, but while I was going to school my only thought was just doing what I had to do to get a good job.

My First Job

My hard work paid off. I got a good job with the Alberta Provincial Government, Dept of Trade and Industry. I worked in the office for two and a half years until I was twenty three years old. At that time Canada was at war so there were many young people joining the armed forces for various reasons; some wanted adventure and excitement, others wanted the experience of doing and seeing something different. I decided to join the armed forces at that time as well for my own reasons, I was patriotic and wanted to serve to help protect my country, and as I had already met two personal goals, my education and a good job, I realized that joining the armed forces would provide me with yet another goal, to travel, especially overseas.

Alberta Women's Service Corps

Previous to signing up with the Army I had been a member of a group in Edmonton called the Alberta Women's Service Corps; we were a part of the Signals Corps. We had about 200 to 250 women and took some basic training in drill and communications of the day such as telegraph key, Morse code, semaphore and letter writing.

Our women's group was a reserve group, much like the regular army reserve. There were other groups such as the one I was a member of that were spread throughout the province since they came into being in 1940. There were other groups in most of the other provinces across Canada. Regular male forces personnel trained us all until the time came when there were enough trained female personnel to form our own staff and training facilities

Canadian Women's Army Corps

I joined the Canadian Women's Army Corps on September 11, 1941 in Edmonton, Alberta. I was assigned my regimental number, and will never forget what it was: W13009. The Alberta Military District was number 13 so all of the regimental numbers of those who enlisted in Alberta would start with W13. We were the very first group of women recruited into the corps, and I was the ninth woman to join this new group. The air force was recruiting other women around the same time, but my group started their training ahead of them because we already had some experience in the drills and communication and were familiar with basic military training.

Below Left: (Left to Right) Isobel Russell, "Pop" Thomson, and Dorothy Chartrand (Bellerose) in 'Alberta Women's Service Corps Uniforms', 1941.
Below Right: Centre, Dorothy Bellerose with some of the #16 Coy CWAC at the Currie Barracks.

Photos courtesy of Dorothy Chartrand (Bellerose)

Photos courtesy of Dorothy Chartrand (Bellerose)
Top Left: Staff Sergeant Dorothy Bellerose
CWAC Barracks, Currie Calgary, 1942.
Top Right: CWAC Quarters, Currie BKS.
Calgary, 1942

"P" Company

Almost immediately after passing my medical with an "A " standing, I joined a group of young women on the train that would take us to Calgary where we would begin our basic training. There were fifteen women from Edmonton and three more from Red Deer who joined us on our trip south. I discovered that many of the girls I met there were from Calgary and rural towns in Alberta. Basic training meant living a different way of life, quite unlike what most of us were used to. We were a large group who had to do everything together, but coming from a large family, sharing quarters in the army barracks with so many girls was not too drastic of a change for me. We were called the "P" Company at first, Edmonton was "Q" Company, and later on we were allotted numbers 2 and 16. We eventually became a company of 87 members.

Official Training

After five hectic weeks of getting our official training and meeting all of the girls in our CWAC company, we were dispatched to work at Mewata Barracks, District Military Headquarters, and some went to supply depots and training centres like the Transport Training Centre in Red Deer, others went to The Prince of Wales Armouries in Edmonton,

Services Corps or to military hospitals. This was to be considered a trial basis and much was expected of us in our deportment and behaviour, both at work and during our leisure time. We had to be top notch in order to meet the standards of camp commandants and superiors, whose mindset was that women did not belong in the Canadian Armed Forces. However we proved ourselves to be the helping hands required. We proved our worth so well that these same people were soon anxious to have more female help, especially in the offices, so the recruiting continued.

The Stylish Uniform

The uniform of the Canadian Women's Army Corps were so stylish. They were made of woollen barathea in khaki, with brown shoulder tabs on the jackets. Skirts were a six-gored A-lined creation, which could not be any higher off the ground than fourteen inches. Caps were of the French Kepi style and the cap badge was diamond shaped. Lisle hose in a beige colour and brown oxford shoes were worn. Nylon hose (a rare thing in those years) were strictly forbidden, as was any bright coloured nail polish. I don't recall any one being disciplined for infraction of those two rules. Face make-up had to be very minimal at all times, and hair had to be off of the collar, if your hair was long it had to be pinned up.

We were also issued summer uniforms of a lighter colour beige material with matching caps. Greatcoats were worn in the winter, and for summer wear, we had an issue of a topcoat in a light shade of beige similar to the all-weather raincoats of today. Our prize issue were the brown glamour boots as we called them; they were four-buckled pull-on overshoes that extended at least nine or ten inches up from the heel. They kept us warm during the cold Canadian winters. Sadly we had to relinquish those from our kit when we proceeded overseas. Instead, we were given time to go to the shoemakers to have an extra thick sole put on our shoes.

First Posting

My first posting lasted for five months in Red Deer, then back to Calgary, where I worked in administration for the women. I was promoted to Cpl. Clerk in the CWAC Administration office in the Mewata Barracks. I then received another promotion; I was designated to supervise the Orderly Room for the CWAC at Currie Barracks. In the summer of 1942, I was promoted to Sergeant then in 1943 I received another

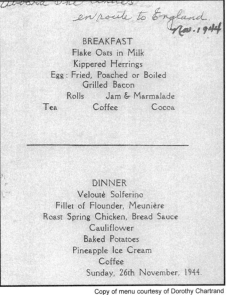

en route to England
Nov. 1944

BREAKFAST
Flake Oats in Milk
Kippered Herrings
Egg : Fried, Poached or Boiled
Grilled Bacon
Rolls   Jam & Marmalade
Tea   Coffee   Cocoa

DINNER
Velouté Solferino
Fillet of Flounder, Meunière
Roast Spring Chicken, Bread Sauce
Cauliflower
Baked Potatoes
Pineapple Ice Cream
Coffee
Sunday, 26th November, 1944.

Copy of menu courtesy of Dorothy Chartrand
Top Left: Trafalgar Square on Victory Day May 1945
Top Right: The Menu aboard the "Andes" enroute to England, November 26, 1944 .

promotion to Staff Sergeant, but that promotion was short lived due to a job becoming available for a steno with a District Education office at District Headquarters in downtown Calgary. It called for a rank of Sergeant, so I relinquished the Staff Sergeant Crown and retained only the three stripes.

After a pleasant working experience there, my name was finally placed on overseas draft. I had seen so many of my army friends go overseas that I was glad to have the opportunity to do the same.

Overseas Duty at Last

I left Calgary on Sept 13, 1944, as a very excited young woman. I went to Kitchener, Ontario to join the overseas group that was being formed at the CWAC basic training centre in Kitchener. Finally, on November 29 1944 we all boarded a troop train that took us to Halifax. Once we arrived there we changed our mode of travel, we got off the train and onto a ship that took us to Liverpool, England. This is an experience I will never forget. It was exciting, educational, and above all, dangerous. I was told there were German submarines in the Atlantic Ocean nearby, I heard the air raid sirens and the explosions of the missiles that were catapulted over to London, from Holland and was very thankful that they were not too close to where I worked.

Prince Charming In a Uniform

I had a lot of friends, but no serious boyfriends. Ten days after my arrival in England, I met my prince charming, Sergeant Robert Atchison. We met at Aldershot in England, County of Hampshire. He was a sergeant in the Medical Corps, but more than that he was also a Canadian. He had grown up on a farm in Saskatchewan.

Photo courtesy of Dorothy Chartrand (Bellerose)

Dorothy Chartrand (Bellerose) and her first husband Sergeant Robert Atchison in 1945.

Every time I went to the Mess hall for my meals I had to walk by his office and he would come to the door and say hello, I didn't know what was happening at the time. He later told me he was laying the groundwork to meet me. Then one Sunday Robert was invited to sit at my table and another Sergeant introduced us. Sunday breakfast was always a special meal because that was when we got to eat real eggs; on other days we had powdered eggs. Robert and I became good friends first, and then our friendship developed into a romance. The Army Chaplain in a small church, not very far from Trafalgar Square, married us on July 26, 1945. It was a small wedding; we both wore our uniforms, as did our two attendants. We went out to dinner with four other military people after the ceremony.

I will never forget my experiences during that year. England is a beautiful country in the spring and summer. The Chestnut trees are gorgeous when they bloom and flowers were everywhere. The winter was bitterly cold, but not much snow, if it did snow it only lasted about twenty-four hours. The rain was different too; they didn't get downpours like we do in Canada. The rain was like a heavy mist and we had a lot of fog.

Coming Home

I remained overseas for just under one year. By that time peace treaties were signed with the German and Japanese people, so I was sent back home to Canada in September 1945, four years after joining the CWAC. My husband Robert returned after six years of service, docking at Quebec City on the Ile de France. I docked at Halifax a few days later on the New Amsterdam.

I was not the only member of my family to join the forces. I had three brothers in active service as well, two in the Army and another in the Navy. We all saw overseas service and we remain forever thankful that we all returned unscathed, and ever so much wiser for our experiences.

I now reside in Edmonton, Alberta. Robert and I had four children, three girls and one boy. Robert passed away in 1958. I later remarried Elie Chartrand in 1963; he too passed away in 1991.

Even today when we hold our CWAC Reunions, many of the dress restrictions are still visible. I have never associated with a friendlier group of women anywhere. We had formed such an "Esprit de Corps" that still remains. The camaraderie among the girls was something I will never forget. I am an active member of the Royal Canadian Legion, Edmonton Ex-Service Women's Branch 215. I presently hold the position of the Sgt.-At-Arms. I wear my War and Legion medals with pride, and on special occasions, I wear my Canadian Volunteer Service Medal with Bar and the 1939-1945 War Medal. I have served as a member of the Legion Colour party for ten years and have participated in many parades in the Edmonton District. I have not missed many Remembrance Day parades over the years.

I remain a proud Canadian Métis woman, who has done service for my country and comrades in many ways, and will continue to do so until my final hours.

PRIVATE MARY CARDINAL

CWAC insignia

Photo courtesy Mary Cardinal

Mary Cardinal in her brand new CWAC
uniform, 1943.

Born a Loner

I was always a loner, but born into a family of eight I would have to go off by myself quite often. I was born at Andrew, Alberta on October 11, 1922. My parents were William James and Mary Cardinal nee Mennie Going off by myself to be alone with nature and my own thoughts were times I fondly remember. One of my favourite ways to be alone was to saddle up my horse and head for the woods. I would usually ride for at least 10 miles at a time. I liked to take my 22 rifle and shoot gophers, I became a deadly shot, the gophers didn't stand a chance. Sometimes when they wouldn't show them selves I would drown them out, shoot them, and give the gopher's tails to my younger brother James to sell. He was saving up to buy a bike.

Andrew was a small community, with mixed farming and various other little industries that the residents worked at to make a living for themselves and their families. I attended the small country school that Andrew afforded. My grandfather Robert Mennie worked hard at the two jobs he had; one as a game warden and the other as a judge. This was his occupation for 45 years. My dad also worked in a different capacity within the justice system. He was a driver who would transport the prisoners to Fort Saskatchewan. When he first started he transported the prisoners by horse drawn wagons and later on he drove them in a panel when cars came available in the 1920's. My dad was one of the people who helped build the jail there and the mental institute in Oliver Alberta as well.

Joining The CWAC

I left school and went to be a mother's helper and babysitter in Lamont and Fort Saskatchewan. I worked on a farm in Willingdon and Pakan, Alberta near Smoky Lake. I enjoyed the housekeeping and especially the cooking. We would put up huge meals to feed the extra farmers that would come to help their neighbours at threshing time. It was there that I decided to join the armed forces. I applied first of all in Edmonton but they would not accept my application due to my weight; the overweight recruiting officer said I was too heavy, I asked her how she got in? I had a lot of spunk back then and I still do, I always say what I want to.

At the age of 21 I joined the Canadian Women's Army Corps in Calgary on July 27, 1943. I was Private Mary Cardinal W130162 and that is the rank I maintained all of the way through my enlistment. I had an opportunity to become a sergeant but I didn't accept the position because I'm not that type, although my dad, sister and my brothers were. They all accepted their promotions when they received them. Altogether there were five of us from my family that joined the army, my dad was in the First and Second World Wars, his name was Sergeant William James Cardinal, and he was wounded at Normandy, France, in World War One. Years later when he was seventy years old he had his leg amputated; it was then that

Below: Private Mary Cardinal and friend, 1943.

Photo courtesy Mary Cardinal

the doctors discovered a piece of shrapnel in the leg he had to lose. My brother Wendell was a sergeant in the military police force and my sister Verna was a Corporal, we had a second brother in the army his name was James. He joined in 1947 and was wounded in Germany, and was sent home. He was killed in a car accident in Ontario the day he got back to Canada. He and a friend were crossing the street when a car went through a red light and killed them both. It was very hard for the family to accept.

Two Choices

I was a very young twenty-one years and more than eager to go and joining the army was not a problem; it was something I was already familiar with as I had been raised in a military atmosphere. When I decided to join up I did so because I only had two choices, either I joined the forces, or I could become a nun. I was not interested in becoming a nun, so I became a soldier.

The CWACs were all issued uniforms and I sure liked what we got. The uniforms were so nice and neat looking. I liked them because I had always worn skirts and shirts to school and around the house at home. I had never worn slacks until I was in the army. We occasionally had to wear white pants for the cooks uniform and shorts when we were in gym. The first time I had to wear shorts in public, I remember I felt naked. I told the sergeant I didn't like them but she said I had to wear them in the gym.

Below: Cooks Trades Training School graduation September 1943. Mary Cardinal is seated on the centre right, front row.

Photo courtesy Mary Cardinal

67

Basic Training

I was immediately sent to Vermillion, Alberta for a 30 day basic training stint. The training was not easy; I remember doing a long 25-mile march one time. We had to go for twelve and a half miles one way then turn around march back to base. Some of the girls were falling over in a faint, and passing out or had terrible blisters and the ambulances had to take them back to the barracks in Vermillion.

Top Left: Mary and friends, Mary is on the right.
Top Right: Mary and friend Margaret Smith ankle deep in snow with two maintence men in Lougheed Barracks, Alberta.
Below: Mary Cardinal in action as a 'cook' in Lougheed Barracks, Alberta.

Photos courtesy Mary Cardinal

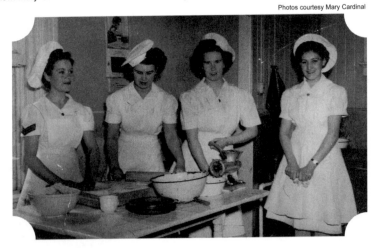

I had just completed basic training and was now on my way back to Currie Barracks in Calgary just as my sister Verna was arriving in Vermillion, so we didn't see much of each other during our time in the army.

Once I got back to Currie, I went to the trades' school and became a cook. There were only twenty-six of us to graduate; the other girls either had chicken pox, measles or mumps. People came from other countries to join the Canadian Army; there was one fellow from Norway and four Americans, who trained to be a cook in the same school as I went to.

I was sent back to Vermillion for six months to cook, until that training centre closed down. While I was in Vermillion, there were approximately 5000 people in the barracks for basic training and we had to cook for all of them. There were 7 platoons when I graduated from trades school, and there were usually 35 to 40 girls in each platoon, but not all of the girls passed the basic training on the first try, some had to repeat the training

There was more than one kitchen that served the large base. My kitchen was number five, A16 CITC C A. We were responsible to cook for the boys who were training to go overseas. Sergeant Lock and I would cook for 500 men at a time. One September we had 1000 men to feed. I worked from 4 am to 12 noon each day with the help of six or seven girls who helped to get the food out and keep the dinning room clean. I enjoyed my work there we had so much fun.

No Discrimination From Our Comrades

There was no discrimination that I was aware of, everybody was treated the same, didn't matter what colour you were. The nicest regiment was the Black Regiment. They were so polite and when you seen them march in a parade; it made you feel like dancing. The first time I met Lieutenant Tess Truman, we were dressed in our brown fatigues. We hit it off right away and ended up wrestling on the floor. We weren't supposed to associate with a higher ranking personal, but we used to say I was her bodyguard when we went into town shopping. The community readily accepted and trusted us, we had one little girl who would come out to play with us whenever we were outside, I can't remember her name.

I will never forget the "Pee Parade" in the town of Vermillion. It was in December I believe, and about forty degrees below Fahrenheit when all of our water pipes froze. I was quite late in the evening about midnight, and no water, or bathrooms. We had to take three truckloads of army personnel into the two hotels in town. There must have been about seven hundred of us in all. Some of us had to walk but we all needed to go so bad that you did what you had to do.

Lougheed Barracks

I was then transferred to Lougheed Barracks in Calgary, where I spent the remainder of my time until my discharge. This house had been the home of Mrs. Lougheed, who was a beautiful tall lady with raven black hair and green eyes. She was as nice to talk to, as she was to look at. She told all the girls who worked there that she was happy we were keeping her home so well. There were French windows in the basement, as well as on the first and second floor. There were two men who kept the outside windows and walks constantly washed and clean. Inside the house

Top Left: Mary Cardinal and friend, Margaret Smith at the Lougheed Barracks, March 1944. According to Mary the little face you see on her left is the face of a little girl that would visit the barracks kitchens regularly. Mary was pleasantly surprised to have a momento of her little friend.
Top Right: Mary Cardinal and friend Sue McMorin having great fun dancing on a tire.

Photos courtesy Mary Cardinal

the girls were constantly polishing this and polishing that, the house was always very clean and sparkling. The cooks lived in the attic and some of the girls lived in the basement, there were six rooms down there with bunk beds. . The officers lived on the second and third floor. The main floor was the kitchen, galley where we washed the pots and pans and the walk in freezer. It was also where the administration work was done, with a living room, dining room and a small canteen, it was a very large house. There were 85 people in all that lived there. It was a lot of hard work but we also had a lot of fun.

We were really an innovative bunch when it came to entertaining ourselves. We usually made up our own games that always turned out to be the greatest fun. I remember dancing on a tire with my girl friend and trying to see who could stay on the longest without falling off. There were 85 of us girls living all together at the time, and we got along quite well. I vividly remember Kotex Day; this day happened on a monthly basis. A crew would come in with many large boxes and they would pass out 12 to each girl.

Sisters In uniform

One night some soldiers threw a naked man into the women's barracks, in Vermillion, we were all screaming and laughing. One of our girls picked him up and threw him out into the snow. I bet he was cold. We were like sisters in uniform and went everywhere in groups, and did all sorts of things together as we were always ready for a bit of fun. In the summertime we would go to the Bowden Park and play lawn golf, it was like miniature golf today, it also had a swinging bridge that I went on and got so scared I had to crawl off of it. The park was close to the river and one Sunday a soldier was coaxing us girls to go for a canoe ride with him. I pretended to get into the boat but instead I tipped it over, and we all ran away laughing. Other times we would go horse back riding, and walk for miles, we'd take a lunch and some times get lost, but we always found our way back. We would go to the movies and dances. One night I gave a fresh Lieutenant a fat lip, his wife came to the barracks looking for me the next day. I went out to meet her and she shook my hand and said, "thank you, he deserved that". Another time I kicked a sailor where it hurts, his friends had to carry him out. They had no right to touch me in wrong places; I didn't join up to be anybody's ground sheet and I let them know it straight off. All of us girls had been taught discipline and learned to respect each other. These men should have respected me the same way.

I had reddish brown hair back then, it was an indication of my temperament when someone got me riled up. My hair colour earned me the nickname of carrot top and that is what people always called me.

Honourable Discharge

I had a lot of friends but no special boyfriends. I didn't meet my husband Alvin Hummel until I got out of the army. I was discharged April 1946. My brother and brothers in law worked in Norman Wells, North West Territories and would bring this fellow home with them, because he was so far away from his family. He came from Ariss Ontario. I sure didn't like him at first, but he was there every weekend so gradually we became friends.

We married on March 05, 1950 in Edmonton, Alberta. We rented a fully furnished house; even the real silverware, lace tablecloths, and bedding were left for our use. The lady had to leave for eighteen months, and she trusted us to look after her home. We left the house repaired and cleaner then when we arrived. The army wanted me to rejoin the forces but I had a baby boy and another on the way. We continued to live in Edmonton for the rest of our married life. We had five children, four boys and one girl. Al was a foreman for the Canadian Pacific Railroad for thirty-five years then he retired. We belonged to the Montgomery Legion Branch 215 and enjoyed going to their banquets and such. We got along very well he became my best friend, oh we had our squabbles, but he always teased me out of them. We were married for forty-six years, one month and fifteen days. He said we would aim for fifty years but he couldn't make it. Al passed away eight years ago. I still manage to live in my own home and tend to my gardens, both vegetables and flowers. I have our children over to visit quite often and enjoy our grandchildren immensely.

The army taught me respect, good manners and courtesy of others and their belongings. I think the discipline was the best, and all of the young people should go for six months basic training. It taught us all to get along with others, no matter what their race or creed. I believe we can make a better world to live in if everyone had respect for each other.

PRIVATE TERESA DION
Achievements of a Young Métis Woman

CWAC insignia

Photo courtesy of Theresa Dion

Theresa Dion, 1942.

Born in the Alberta Sunshine

Northern Alberta is the land of my birth, I was born there in Gunn, Alberta during in the twenties. I lived with my family on a farm that was located one mile from the Fern Valley School. My earliest memories include walking to and from school throughout the year; my most vivid memories are about the winter weather that was at times 40 below Fahrenheit. There were no school buses to pick up any children at that time so we all trekked over and through snow that could sometimes be waist deep, on our daily journey to and from the little country school. Roads were not ploughed in those days and the wind always had a will of it's own; one that it exercised frequently; so noticeably especially during the winter months. We would often find the wind had caused the snow to drift in a way that would create mounds and dips that made walking quite difficult. On some days the snow drifted over the fence posts, a blessing in disguise, as we could use this situation to our advantage, we found the walking was easier up there above the roadway because that's where the snow was packed the best.

As a child I enjoyed the winter weather; and if I listen carefully I can still hear the crispy tinkle of the snow as it sparkled out loud when our feet crushed through the millions of tiny diamonds that were made of ice and crystal. I remember how they danced so brilliantly under the clear blue sunny Alberta skies of my youth.

New Years Day

The most exciting day of the year was New Years Day. Ma would prepare food all week for the visitors that always came to share this special annual event in our lives. All of us children would be up and keen to get the day started by four a.m. For this exceptional, splendid day we would all be dressed in our new clothes; I would always have a new dress and my two brothers would have new pants and shirts that ma had made just for us.

Even at that early hour, Ma would have the table set and food ready when we arrived in the kitchen for our breakfast. Dad would be all dressed up in his finest suit waiting for the family to gather so we could kneel down in front of him and receive the blessings he would give us. We would then sit down to a wonderful breakfast that had been prepared with love and care; those mornings were among the best ever. As soon as breakfast was over we would hurry to tidy the kitchen, wash the dishes and reset the table for the guests who would soon arrive.

The excitement and expectations we were filled with was enhanced greatly by the sounds of happy voices calling to the house. The sounds of the bells on the horses echoed through the cold winter air as they ran down the lane toward our home. The teams of horses would be pulling sleighs that were filled with our Métis friends and relatives who were making a round of calls to visit with and wish the elders a good year and receive their blessings in turn. This went on all morning and into the afternoon, people coming, people going and everyone greeting each other with a kiss and handshake, laughing, talking and eating.

When the last sleigh load pulled away from our house, dad would then hitch up our team of horses to the sleigh and Ma would have some hot rocks in the bottom of the box. My brothers would fill it with sweet smelling hay and we would go out to make our own rounds from house to house to visit our Elders, to receive their blessings. We were welcomed in all the homes we stopped at in much the same way my family had welcomed every visitor that had been to our house earlier in the day. We would make our rounds until the early evening when we would go to the home that belonged to whoever's family that would be having a "New Years Day party" to celebrate the new one just coming in. For many of us the end of the wonderful day of visiting meant the begining of the best that was yet to come. As each wagon turned to head in the same direction everyone's senses became alert with the anticipation of the fun to come.

We would arrive at the house where the party was to take place to find that the family had taken out all of the furniture from the largest room in the house, usually the living room and stored it in the other rooms or outside in the warehouses. As the families arrived people greeted each other as though months instead of hours had passed since their last meeting. The women would hurry in with bundled babies and what ever food they could bring for the lunch. The men rushed to unhitch the teams from the wagons, give each horse some hay and dash into the house to help finish the final work that had to be done so the music and dancing could start.

As they arrived, the musicians would take their seats and begin to tune up their instruments. The house was soon filled with the sounds of fiddles and guitars that urged everyone to tap their feet. What music they made, it was impossible to keep still. Infants and toddlers were placed in a corner of the room where all could carefully watch them; and when the little ones needed to sleep they were snuggled into blankets that had been placed on the floor behind the musicians. I remember one evening when a grandmother laid a tiny sleeping girl gently into an open guitar case. She stayed sleeping there snug, warm and secure until it was time to go home. Young and old would join in the dancing, no one was left standing, not even those who were a little unsure of themselves as the elders made sure we all took part in dancing and learned the traditional dances that included intricate reels, elegant waltzes and always the Red River Jig. This was our custom, that what you did on New Years day would be the example of the days to come, so being happy was very important.

Frozen Bannock Sandwiches

With the New Years celebrations over, it meant going back to school. We had to wear many layers of very warm clothing, especially in that kind of weather as it took a lot to stay warm. We only had one room in our school - house, so all grades were taught together. The different grades were divided into rows within the room instead of by separate rooms as they are today. The teachers had to do everything involved with being a country school teacher; they had to go outside to supervise and referee sports and play at recess and lunchtime. They also spent a lot of time in the community fundraising, usually by organizing family dances in order to have enough money to ensure the school children would have enough books and supplies, a Christmas concert and a bag of candy with a sweet orange from Santa Clause for everyone.

During the coldest months the teachers helped us arrange our desks as close as possible around the wood-burning furnace vent to keep us from freezing and help make us more comfortable. The furnace only had one large vent and barely managed to keep the room above freezing on some days. But it prevented anyone from getting frostbite as lessons were taught and learned; but most of all, we would place our lunches on the ledge and it ensured a temperature that would thaw the frozen bannock sandwiches that would be our lunch. The older boys fed the furnace split wood blocks on a regular basis to ensure our fingers stayed warm enough to write. I know life was difficult during the 1930's in Alberta, but memory is a wonderful thing as it is able to lift and uphold all of the shining, positive and excellent experiences of childhood in a way that allows us to mainly remember the good parts.

I completed my ninth year of school by correspondence at Fern Valley. The next year I went to Edmonton where I continued my secondary education at St. Mary's High School. I was from another school district so this meant I had to pay tuition. I was also responsible for paying my room and board so I worked for the family I lived with to help meet my financial needs. The family was very religious and that meant I also had to attend church every single morning at 6 am. I continued working, going to church and attending classes until I completed grade 11, but it was quite a struggle and too much of a financial burden so I had to quit. It broke my heart to do so as I had wanted so badly to complete my high school education. Completing grade 11 was quite an achievement for a Métis Woman at that time and that level of education helped me get a good job in the forces later on in my life.

Enlisting in the CWAC

In 1942, I was a very young eighteen year old, and as green as a sapling in May when I enlisted with the Canadian Women Army Corps (CWAC) in Edmonton and was assigned my number, W13859. Aside from wanting to do my patriotic duty; a feverish excitement that was a part of the young people at the time; I wanted passionately to go overseas to see what the war was really like. It was a scary but exciting time for me and I wanted to be a part of the action. In spite of my determination and ideals I was never given permission to go overseas. I was aware at the time that all of the women I knew who wanted to go overseas were denied permission and had to stay in Canada; all were my friends and comrades on the home front. I know that other women were given the privilege to serve overseas, but to the best of my knowledge none of them were Aboriginal women. I also believe that another reason I was denied overseas duty is because I was only eighteen at the time I applied, I was simply just too young.

I was looking for an new experience with war time action, but wouldn't you know it the first thing that happened when I enlisted in Edmonton, I found I would have to stay there for a while because we were quarantined for two weeks because one of the girls in my platoon got the measles; not my idea of defending my country in a heroic and glorious way. I got through it by getting to know my fellow captives and finding out that they were all a lot like me; this experience forged a bond for all of us who had been confined together during that time. After the quarantine was over, I was transferred to Vermillion, Alberta where I completed my basic training over a period of three months. What a time that was. It took skill, heart, brains and determination to get through it, many of us did and there were some who didn't. To this day I am proud that I was one of who not only made it, but also excelled.

No Discrimination in the Service

I didn't feel any discrimination while I was in the service as there was no time for that kind of thing until afterwards. I believe I experienced a subtle form of discrimination that was practiced at the time as I was not offered the information on any veteran's benefits or of the Veterans Land Act that would have entitled me to own land; during or after the war, and by the time I found out and applied for the benefits I was told that they were discontinued.

High-Security-Secrecy

With basic training complete I was moved around from station to station throughout Alberta. I stayed in Alberta the whole time at experimental stations. Although my entire time in the service was spent within the province, I did not at any time ever know when or where I was being transferred. Due to the nature of my work everything was done under high-security-secrecy. Canada was training ground for armament chemicals, so people from many other countries came here to take the training our country offered.

My work included a lot of Administration - Office duties at the various stations in Edmonton, Calgary and Suffield. There were a lot of vacancies in this area as men had previously filled them; now it was the woman's role to work in these positions so the men would be free to go overseas. The work was demanding and sometimes tedious for all the girls; but overall we really had very good times together while we were in the forces. We did a lot of the silly things that young people do.

Good Times

There were many good times that I fondly remember. The nicest time of all was when I met and soon after married John Ewachewski. We were posted at the Suffield Experimental Station near Medicine Hat. We met casually and got along so well together that we did not need a long engagement to know we wanted to spend the rest of our lives together. We were married soon after we met in 1944.

I remember so well the day he became my husband, it was such a hurried and wonderful affair. We were married at 2 o'clock in the afternoon and he got shipped out at 6 o'clock the same day. The honeymoon was much shorter than the courtship. He was sent to protect the home front on the DEW line in the Northwest Territories. I would not see this man that I had fallen in love with and married so quickly for two years, when the war was over. This lifestyle did not allow me to make any lasting friendships. Whenever I made friends, I soon lost track of them. It was a lonely and frustrating experience, but it was wartime and everything was so intense that it gave me a powerful sense of duty and service that helped me to overcome the feelings of loneliness and frustrations that I felt.

We Were All So Young Then

We were stationed out in the country, and there were lots of interesting things for us to do. The entertainment was good and went a long way to make sure we did not get into mischief; we were all so young then. We had dances and bike rides, sometimes we would ride out of bounds into the experimental areas, where we weren't supposed to go but we never got caught. We had wonderful ball games in the summer when the girl's team would play other girls teams from different stations; I loved to play ball at every chance I got. We were also provided with a skating rink in the winter. The boys who played hockey used the rink while the girls watched on, as girls didn't play hockey in those days. Everyone skated together when the boys weren't playing hockey. There was also transportation available, a bus would take us into town and back when we had weekend passes and most of us went as it was a nice change of pace. Of course there were the ever present duties that was part of army life which meant we marched in a lot of parades and were subject to constant inspections. We would march for miles. It was very hard at first, until I got used to it. It must have been good for me because it was the healthiest I have ever felt in my life.

Families Joined Up

I didn't have to go to the front lines like brother George Dion did. He went overseas and afterwards all he would say about his experiences was that "War was very bad". His memories bothered him and he didn't like to talk about it. Families would join up, I had two brothers in the army, my brother Eddy Dion was kept in Canada at Williams Lake, B.C., but George went through the whole campaign in England, Africa, Italy, France, Belgium, Holland and Germany. I don't agree with war either; there are other ways to bring peace without having a war

Excellent Training and Experience

I wasn't very worldly, coming from a farm into the city, so the army gave me a good education, more than academics. I gained more of a focus on what I wanted to do later in life. I met people from other countries who came to take training in Canada that gave me a broader view of people and how to interact with them. As a result of the experience and training I got in the Army, I gained a lot of self-confidence, by proving to myself what I could do. I worked for Revenue Canada-Data Base when I was discharged. My husband and I also ran our own business for 31 years. He was a wonderful person and husband who was very good to me. We had two children and later two grandchildren. We had a good long marriage until he passed away a few years ago; he was always my best friend.

In 1972 we moved to British Columbia where I still reside. I am an active community member volunteering my time working with children in the school district; I am a member of the Aboriginal Veterans Committee, and Métis Children's Society board member. I am also the Assistant Curator at the Michief Cultural Historical Society where I teach Métis dancing to the children. I am recognized as a Métis Elder in my community. I feel I have gained many positive experiences from my time in the Army, that now I am able to continue my life as a productive citizen of the country that so many people fought so hard to keep free!

REFERENCES

Barron Norris, Marjorie
>Sister Heroines: The Roseate Glow of Wartime Nursing 1914 - 1918; Bunker to Bunker Publishing; 2002.

Byfield, Ted
>Alberta in the 20th Century: Volume Eight, the War That United the Province 1939 - 1945; United Western Communications Ltd.; 2000.

Drinkwater, Catherine K.
>Letters to Edgewood Farm: From a Canadian Girl in World War II; Bunker to Bunker Publishing; 2002.

Calahoo Women's Institute
>Mrs. K. Dalheim, Editor; Mrs. M. Kerr, Co-editor; Calahoo Trails;

Colchester Women's Institute
>Down Memory Lane in Colchester, Glenbow Alberta Institute; 1980.

Forgotten Warrior: National Aboriginal Veterans Magazine; "Old Guard". Volume 1, Issue 1, August - September

Granfield, Linda
>Brass Buttons and Silver Horseshoes: Stories from Canada's British War Brides; McClelland & Stewart Ltd, The Canadian Publishers; 2002

Klein, Mary
>Ten Dollars and a Dream; L.I.F.E. History Committee; 1977.

Kuhn, Edgar A.
>Ellesmere Land: A Mountie in the High Arctic; Bunker to Bunker Publishing, 2002.

Tingley, Ken Editor
> **For King and Country: Alberta in the Second World War**; The
> Provincial Museum of Alberta, Reidmore Books Inc.; 1995.

Tribal Chiefs Institute and Indian and Northern Affairs
> **In Their Footsteps: Contributions of First Nations People in
> Alberta**; Tribal Chiefs Institute of Treaty 6; 2001.

OUR WOMEN IN UNIFORM
STEERING COMMITTEE

Photo courtesy the Institute for the Advancment of Aboriginal Women

Steering Committee
Back row: P. Gayle McKenzie - Lead Researcher/ Writer (Gunn), Donald Langford - Vice-President Aboriginal Veterans Society of Alberta (Edmonton), Jan Roseneder - Military History Librarian Museum of Regiments (Calgary), Ginny Belcourt Todd - Writer (Gunn).
Front row: Bertha Clark Jones - IAAW Elder Veteran Air Force (Athabasca), Muriel Stanley-Venne - President & Founder of the Institute for the Advancement of Aboriginal Women (Edmonton).

Below Left: Victor Letendre - President Aboriginal Veterans Society of Alberta (Edmonton).
Below Right: Honourary Committee Member: Senator Thelma Chalifoux (St. Albert).